TAKE RISK!

To my beloved family and friends who stood by us all
and provided the support which made all this possible.

With very grateful thanks.

TAKE
RISK!

RICHARD NOBLE

EVRO
PUBLISHING

Published in April 2020

ISBN 978-1-910505-51-9

Published by Evro Publishing, Westrow House, Holwell, Sherborne, Dorset DT9 5LF

Printed and bound in Malta by Gutenberg Press

Every effort has been made to trace and acknowledge holders of copyright in photographs and to obtain their permission for the use of photographs. The publisher apologises for any errors or omissions in the credits given throughout this book and would be grateful to be notified of any corrections that should be incorporated in future reprints or editions.

www.evropublishing.com

CONTENTS

INTRODUCTION

This was never going to be a normal book. It was always going to be different. This is not the story of projects and project team members. It is the story of the amazingly brave people who took risks to back us and the extraordinary twists and turns of the maze of opportunities that enabled our successes and brought about our failures. And, of course, you learn much more from failure.

I come from an extraordinary age. It was a time in the 1950s when Britain led the world, when brilliant and risk-taking engineers force-fed on the high-pressure demands of World War Two engineering just continued the development pace to face up to the appalling challenges of the Cold War. The country led the world in aerospace with the first jet airliners, the manufacture of the most advanced jet engines and very soon record-holding aircraft capable of twice the speed of sound. The austerity of the war was over and, despite the difficult times, the country was looking forward to an amazing future.

It was even safe — because against all the odds we had developed our own nuclear deterrent.

Would the country be able to continue the pace or would we burn out and pass the leadership to larger economies? We are British — we try very hard.

I had seen John Cobb's innovative jet boat *Crusader* on Loch Ness as he headed for 250mph on water in 1952. I had been present at the Farnborough Air Show and seen the Lightning fighters head for the sky at 50,000ft a minute in full afterburner and with a massive roar that echoed around the surrounding hills. Electric guitars were enabling culture-changing rock music and pop stars were earning more than senior civil servants. In 1961 Britain had announced the amazingly beautiful 150mph Jaguar E-type, the car Enzo Ferrari wished he had manufactured.

All this was happening in Britain — so Britain had to be very special.

I left school in the 1960s and wanted to play my part

in this amazing country that welcomed innovation and engineering on such a scale and took incredible risk. The big question we all had was — how do we start? How do you get to take part in all this?

Of course, I was soon to discover that there are checks and balances to make unusual activity very difficult, put in place by rational people with safe and valuable careers. Guardians of society who prevent exposure to risk, rational people who expect predictable and rational behaviour from the young. Unfortunately, this selfish and short-sighted culture reduces innovation and opportunity for everyone.

The important strategy, of course, is to take risk, to become familiar with risk and to know how to deal with it. Ignoring risk leads to backsliding, complacency and failure.

So how to get started?

My father was an army officer who had fought in the World War Two front line since 1939. He banked with Williams & Glyn's in Whitehall — that should be the place to start. The manager took the decision for me: he wanted to discuss my overdraft and total lack of collateral.

The manager, a kindly career banker, asked the question:

"Well, Mr Noble what do you want to do with your life?"

"I'm going to break the World Land Speed Record…"

This was a sensible approach. The Land Speed Record involves outrageous speed where cars go faster than low-level aeroplanes. It involves jet engines, innovation and advanced engineering. It wasn't dependent on government contracts and approval by the risk-adverse brethren.

As you might expect, the banker was both appalled and negative. He saw the world record as an expensive vanity project only available to the very rich.

"May I suggest a very good career in insurance? I have very good contacts."

Of course, he had a very valid point. Past British Land Speed Record heroes had been able to garner substantial funds from their 'aristo' mates — and I had an overdraft. I would have to make up the discrepancy with hard marketing, hard sales drive, nerve and humour.

The banker would have been even more appalled when my first jet car emerged 10 years later, sponsored by the very same bank.

And that's what made all this possible for our people — financial sponsorship. A system that rewards media exposure with funds and allowed our small teams to innovate, take risk and to deliver the most amazing, innovative, safe products completely independently from the rational, risk-adverse establishment. We were all setting out to continue what had been started in 1950s Britain.

It is important to understand that these innovative projects seldom operate in clear financial water. Working an innovative programme against the prevailing culture will always lead to very high levels of stress and total financial unpredictability. To succeed, the project has to have a brazen culture of truth.

I warned you this is going to be a very unusual book. It is about the brave companies and people who shackled themselves to our projects, who made the key decisions to support us with their budgets, often putting their careers on the line in the process — and they made it all possible.

And the most important catalysts in all this? An amazing collective sense of humour and downright team determination as we found ourselves in the most incredible situations.

We have tried very hard and it's not over yet — there is much more to come!

Enjoy!

CHAPTER 1
THRUST 1

"The French are my best customers — if they saw that jet engine and couldn't have it..."

Fred Watson

My elderly aunt Bua, a splendidly upright and focused relative who drove her large Ford car like a bomber pilot over the target, had been persuaded that I needed a respectable car. It was very kind of her because this loan was actually the proxy for my first jet engine. The car didn't remain with me long after I met Fred Watson.

Fred ran a large aero-engine storage and dismantling operation in Portsmouth. In fact he was repurposing the Royal Air Force, which was upgrading from its fleet of some 300 Meteor fighters. Fred had just acquired a large stock of Meteor jet engines — 30 Rolls-Royce Derwent 8s were in his yard.

The Derwent 8, named after the beautiful Derbyshire

river, was an ideal first jet engine. Being centrifugal, it had a big girth and it didn't need an intake; it was light in weight and simple to install; its electrics were straight-forward and it could be started with a couple of large 12-volt truck batteries. Once you had the engine, securing the bits that made it work should have been simple.

Like everything in aviation, it wasn't.

Fred was interested and suggested I check the engines and logs. There was one exceptional one with flying time left on it.

"It's got to be that one, Fred!"

"I would love to help you but the problem is the French."

"The French?"

"The French are my best customers. They fly Meteors round their Pacific atoll nuclear test sites and they will be here on Friday. If they saw that engine and couldn't have it…"

"But Fred, today is Tuesday."

"OK, OK… but it must be gone by tomorrow."

Another relation lent me his farm truck overnight and — *zut alors!* — the Derwent was repositioned in Thames Ditton!

The first car was to be no more than a jet engine,

four wheels, a seat and a bit of fancy bodywork. The idea was to learn the business from the absolute basics and as quickly as possible. The hard bit was the chassis ladder frame on which all this was to be mounted.

The long-term marketing strategy was to pay off well. I had managed to get a job selling building materials around the world for the huge GKN Group. This was an undercover entry into one of the country's largest engineering groups where 60 per cent of the group revenue came from automotive parts — an obvious main sponsor for later but for now we needed the chassis frame.

By chance, the GKN chassis factory was in Telford and the production director was enthusiastic. Together we went around the production line: chassis frames for Land Rover Defenders and Triumph TR6 sports cars — but nothing was remotely suitable. We took a short cut back to the main office via the R&D department.

As soon as we opened the door, we saw the chassis, lying in the dust and covered in engineering dirt and debris — clearly not an urgent job.

"You've found it!"

"Oh, I don't know about that Richard. It's a one-off development piece… must have cost us a bloomin' fortune."

"Does it help if it's 18 inches too long?"

The executive decision took microseconds.

"Come over here, George, and please bring the oxy torch!"

Within seconds the chassis had been burned to length. There was a note of triumph in his voice.

"You can have it now — it's damaged!"

Two days later the chassis joined the Derwent in Thames Ditton. These were the first parts of *Thrust1*.

The word 'Thrust' is a happy coincidence. For the serious aero engineer, it describes the push developed by a jet engine and is measured in pounds. For the less observant marketing executive, it can allude to an intense personal biological activity between consenting adults. We found both groups highly appreciative of the name. So the Derwent car became *Thrust1*.

Of course, *Thrust1* was dangerous: there was no engineering input other than positioning essential components in the most sensible places.

Mid-construction, we had to move *Thrust1* on its wheels to Turnham Green, a leafy London suburb where I shared a flat and a garage. The GKN Maidenhead office caretaker agreed to give up his early Sunday morning to tow *Thrust1* on the main road at 6.00am.

Of course, we were stopped by a sole policeman

completing his shift.

"What in God's name is that?"

"Officer, it's a jet car, the first stage of a World Land Speed Record programme."

"Is it safe?"

"As long as the jet engine isn't running!"

"OK, then get on your way to Turnham Green, don't start it up… and you never met me on the way."

"OK, Officer!"

Sergeant Jim Matthews at RAF St Athan was the man of the moment. In those days the British weather was entirely predictable and winter meant heavy snow and closed runways — not acceptable in the Cold War when everything was on alert. Given their large numbers of Meteor fighters, the Royal Air Force came up with a fine off-the-wall piece of agricultural engineering. The snow-blow units consisted of a wide chassis pushed ahead by a huge fuel tanker; two Derwents were mounted backwards on the chassis together with a small control hut and the hot jet engine exhausts melted and blew away snow, ice and anything in its path. The idea was that the tanker was to push the snow-blow ahead. In fact the engines were so powerful that progress was often difficult, for the tanker often found itself going backwards.

Jim Matthews was the last serving Derwent specialist in the Royal Air Force and we needed his help to get *Thrust1* started. We had proven the starting system in the garage driveway in Turnham Green and terrified the neighbours. Now we had to fuel it and light it up.

Jim and the station commander agreed the plan and we delivered *Thrust1* to RAF St Athan for checking. Jim was a bit surprised by this strange mix of aero and truck engineering but understood the reasoning and was prepared to have a go.

"Come back next week."

We were back the next weekend.

"How did we do, Jim?"

"You didn't do badly but you left out an important part."

We had failed to understand the jet engine drainage system. The great Frank Whittle had learned the important lesson; if the engine does not light up first time, fuel can collect inside and the next start can be highly entertaining. Jim had kindly sorted the drains.

Thrust1 was chained down and we were ready to go.

"Do you want to start it, Jim?"

"No, Richard. You built it, you start it…"

I sat in the cockpit, took instruction from Jim and pushed the start button. This wound up the starter clock and the engine began its sequence, first rotating the compressor slowly and then fast as it gained confidence. The torch igniter and pumps commenced and at a signal from Jim, I opened the high-pressure cock — there was a massive rumble as the fuel went in and the Derwent came to life with the usual smell of part-burned jet fuel. There were no leaks — and the noise was incredible. *Thrust1* was a goer. It was one hell of a moment.

Which was just as well, as the BBC *Tomorrow's World* team were down to film for the next day. This was a change for them — they had been filming a troubling and complicated programme on schizophrenia. I asked the producer how it had gone:

"I am in two minds about it."

So we spent the Sunday with the BBC crew and its great presenter, Raymond Baxter. We took many shots of *Thrust1* trundling up and down the St Athan runway. Baxter was generous enough to state in his commentary that *Thrust1* was just the small beginning of something big.

Thrust1 was never a safe vehicle. We did demonstrations at air shows and at Brands Hatch, where I drove it around the circuit to great enthusiasm and nearly asphyxiated the team in the chase car behind. But the immediate focus was the British Land Speed Record — we needed 200mph.

At that time a new British motorway, the M11, was about to be opened and the concrete surface was ideal. Dunlop were happy with the tyres, the RAC could do the timing, but would the Department of Transport agree to let us use it? We presented in Whitehall and the answer was a firm negative — they were worried that the jet exhaust would melt the tarmac joints between the concrete road slabs and they wouldn't budge. A runway was needed.

Amazingly, we got the use of a runway. RAF Fairford was about to have its runway resurfaced, so repairs were funded if anything went wrong with *Thrust1*. It had been a long, arduous fight, involving getting documentation to civil servants in curious locations at 3am so I could get to work in the GKN Maidenhead office in time.

The car had been lowered so it was no longer the 'Cathedral on Wheels' we had always joked about. There was to be no sleep the night before the run because the borrowed Land Rover tow truck wouldn't couple with the borrowed trailer. Eventually a car-recovery specialist arrived at 3am with truck and trailer and we were on our way to Fairford.

The first run was a delight. *Thrust1* accelerated very smoothly and very fast, probably reaching around 200mph.

I turned the car around and gave it full power... and something gave... and with the huge gyro forces from the rotating masses in the engine the car leapt into the air and went through a triple airborne roll before crashing back on the runway with an almighty smash.

The problem with a jet or rocket car is that if it leaves the ground, it will still keep going in the air — after all the engine comes from an aeroplane and doesn't turn the wheels. I was very calm as we went through all this and got the engine shut down on the first roll.

Sally, my long-suffering wife, was in the fire truck and witnessed the appalling crash and the dense smoke that came from the remains of *Thrust1*.

"Don't you worry," the fireman said as they raced to the scene. "It's only white smoke — there's no fire!"

We scooped up the remains of *Thrust1* and put it on the trailer. The sensible thing to do was for us all to go to the pub. We realised that *Thrust1* wasn't going to teach us any more. On the way home we found a local scrapyard that was still open and traded the remains of *Thrust1* for £175 — so the project remained solvent.

The scrappie was delighted with his purchase.

"We'll soon get that big ol' jet engine running."

When I explained that the engine was shock-loaded and the ignition system could kill him, he gave it second thoughts.

We had learned the lessons from *Thrust1*. It was now time to progress to something much faster.

They started resurfacing the entire Fairford runway the next day — we had only ever had a one-day window.

CHAPTER 2
THRUST 2

"The speed is, for the mile, 642.971mph
— it's a new record. Congratulations!"

Don MacGregor, United States Auto Club

John Ackroyd, a tall, outspoken engineer with a home on the Isle of Wight and a broad sense of humour, was angry. This was because of a small feature we had managed to sneak into the *Daily Telegraph* national newspaper — 'Wanted: 650mph car designer' — along with a list of supporting companies; the giant Lucas Industries had supplied two metres of cable and a switch and of course that qualified them for inclusion as a sponsor...

Engineers from all over the country had applied with spectacular CVs and equally spectacular financial demands — and at about that time GKN sent me to the Far East.

Ackroyd was angry because he had applied and I

hadn't responded.

"What sort of an organisation is this? I applied three weeks ago and didn't even get an answer?"

The sensible thing to do was to put Ackroyd in touch with Ken Norris for an interview. Ken was the designer of Donald Campbell's *Bluebird* K7 Water Speed Record boat and the *Bluebird* CN7 Land Speed Record car. I suddenly got snowed under with GKN work and failed to brief Ken until the next morning.

"Ken, good morning. I have heard from John Ackroyd and suggested he make contact with you for an interview…"

"Richard, he's already here — first thing this morning! He wants to know how much money you have?"

We have just over £160…

"OK — he wants to make a start right away!"

Amazingly the system had thrown up a brilliant, very demanding engineer and a lifelong friend. It was the start of an incredible partnership.

At about this time I had been invited to a meeting with the RAF's Director of Public Affairs. The *Thrust1* episode had generated valuable publicity for the RAF at a time when it seemed to be struggling to generate any media interest in its activities. Nobody wanted to be reminded about the awful Cold War.

Paddy Hine, the director, came straight to the point.

"You want to break the World Land Speed Record? How can we help?"

"We need a Lightning fighter — the upper engine installation and all the fittings."

The timing was right. The RAF was scrapping its Lightning fighters and some were being used as airfield decoys. I ended up borrowing funds and buying a Lightning Avon 210 jet engine for £500. There was one hell of a story about obtaining the last serviceable jet-pipe and afterburner unit that someone had conveniently dropped on the floor at an RAF station but now we had a 25ft engine and some 35,000 horsepower.

The next part of the story belongs to David Benson, long-serving motoring correspondent for the *Daily Express* and the man who helped Donald Campbell into his K7 boat on that fateful day in 1967. He turned up at our home in Twickenham to meet the team. He was evidently impressed.

"We have some space going at the new *Daily Express* Motorfair car show at Earls Court in London."

"Great — we'll put on a stand — we need the public exposure."

"How much space do you need?"

"Well, we have a 25-foot jet engine for a start, so let's say 1,000 square feet."

Thanks to David, we actually got 1,000 square feet on the upper floor of Earls Court. The team from GKN Mills under George Myers designed the huge, professional stand and the scaffolders built it. Our friends at Thames Television guaranteed television coverage. Key to the success was our copy of the 16mm film *The Fastest Man on Earth* and a massive amplification system that meant we could fill the whole of Earls Court with the sound of jet engines, rockets, crashes and American cheering with absolutely outstanding narration by Robert Vaughn, *The Man from U.N.C.L.E*. The stand was run by Alan Bruford, my brother-in-law, who endured 160 hours of the film as it repeatedly ran to huge audiences all jammed into the stand. And, of course, there were many complaints, particularly from the Coldstream Guards Band who were performing on the ground floor and were unable to hear themselves play. A total of 35,000 people crammed into the stand over 13 days.

But the big story was that, on the press day, John Ackroyd wanted Tube Investments, makers of the famous Reynolds 531 chrome-moly-steel tube, to build the huge 3D spaceframe for the car. John Newble, the company's head of public relations, was the man. He decided he was coming on press day. Newble was late and the stand was a huge success with hundreds of people on the stand watching the amazing film. Close up, the noise was incredible. I needed support and Ken Norris kindly gave up his time — this was the now-or-never starter deal.

Newble eventually showed, surrounded by a retinue of Tube Investments and PR people, and was clearly impressed with what he saw. The meeting was short and I was worried that he might drift away without consummating the marriage, so I invited the whole lot to lunch at one of the expensive Earls Court restaurants. Ken worked wonders telling them about Donald Campbell and at the end Newble agreed to build the frame.

Lunch cost the project £65. The TI team had eaten the project's entire working capital but we had a designer, an engine, a supporters' club of hundreds, massive PR and a huge spaceframe to be built by the best frame man in the country, the legendary Ken Sprayson.

We were clearing up after the last night of the show. It was my job to take the huge jet engine home and once outside in the snow I hoisted the two-tonne combination of engine and its stand on one of the Earls

Court manual hoists... and the hoist jammed, leaving our precious engine swinging in the snowstorm 15 feet up. Absolutely nothing is predictable in record-breaking. But against all the odds we had achieved a huge success.

A few days later I was on the Isle of Wight with John Ackroyd. We had rented a derelict kitchen at Ranelagh Works for £5 a week and John had installed himself with the largest drawing board I had ever seen.

"There it is, Richard — the first part of *Thrust2*!"

John held up a small part about the size of a teacup, freshly plated in yellow cadmium.

"What is it, John?"

"It's a fuel tank vent."

And that was where the *Thrust2* build started...

It was March 1978 when John decided to build the *Thrust2* driver's seat. The BBC filmed him pouring the foaming mixture into the seat box around my back and nether regions.

"You've had it now, Richard. You can never change shape..."

We had no idea of the enormous consequences of this innocent bit of filming.

Tony Waring was a director of the laundry group

Initial Services. He needed substantial publicity to expand the business and was finding it hard going. Successful promotion of washrooms and laundries is probably as hard as it gets.

By sheer chance he saw the BBC *Tomorrow's World* seat feature and made his way to the Isle of Wight. Initial Services was to become the project's main sponsor — but the first-stage British Airways story would come first.

It is important to understand how the project survived the early days. It had minimal money, no reputation — and after the Donald Campbell experience sponsors were unsure. The sponsor hunt was never-ending and every lead had to be followed. The project also had to present at multiple shows and exhibitions and demonstrate great quality and professionalism. Mike Collen's company, Marcom of Twickenham, joined the project providing audio-visual equipment and support whenever needed and this dependable background involvement was absolutely vital in building public engagement and branding.

As the project design developed, British Airways began to show solid interest and in due course this developed into the most incredible deal. They were prepared to put in a small sum and wanted the dramatic tailfin for their distinctive logo. There was a problem: the BA logo wouldn't fit John's supersonic tailfin design. John had a quick answer: tell them we'll switch to a Boeing 747 tailfin. This was duly done and when the huge TI spaceframe was shown for the first time, it was accompanied by models exhibiting the BA logo on the 747 tailfins.

The response was immediate: BA's Head of Operations from Manchester was on the phone as soon as the frame footage went out.

"How dare you use the British Airways logo on your car tail — you can get into real trouble for this."

"You see — it really works!"

"What do you mean?"

"Well, British Airways is our first sponsor — and it's got to you!"

In fact the first BA relationship didn't last long — but the most amazing relationship was to save the project later.

We showed the huge car as a rolling skeleton at the Tower Hotel in London to huge acclaim, particularly to the beautiful lady model in the *Thrust2* T-shirt that TI had thoughtfully sent along to offset the image of the hairy engineers.

Shortly after that the project ran out of money. We

had the car on its wheels and it was going to run at air shows in 1980 — it was a considerable achievement. But we were out of money. We sat with the sponsors in the Cumberland Hotel in Whitehall and one by one they made their apologies and left. Fortunately we didn't have to pay for the use of the room.

Two days later Richard Chisnell from Initial Services was on the phone.

"Glad to report that the Initial Board has decided to double up on the sponsorship — just keep going!"

The arrangement I had with my employer, GKN Mills, was that since I spent so much time abroad, they would allow me to use the office phone to further the project. One morning I was in my office trying to finalise a major deal with a main board member of the would-be sponsor on the line — this was my chance to land the deal after months of patient development. As the conversation progressed, in walked the GKN Mills Managing Director, Bill Orwin. I had to keep going otherwise I would lose the deal. Orwin wasn't going to go away — he stood with his back to me looking out of the window as I closed the deal. I was red-faced with embarrassment.

"Well, Richard, how's it all going?"

"Well, we are doing well in Hong Kong with the floor moulds and it does look as though we have made the breakthrough with steel access scaffolding in Shell Brunei..."

Orwin's response was memorable.

"Not that crap. Richard. The car! How's it going?"

It was 1980, a crucial year. John Ackroyd was concerned that the car was nearly ready for its UK runway displays at air shows and I was still selling GKN building materials around the world. Time to move on, so I wrote to the GKN boss, Roy Roberts, eight layers of GKN management above me.

Dear Mr Roberts,
I am sorry that I am unable to give you my contractual notice but the Land Speed Record car is now ready for UK trials and I have to go and do the driving.
PS: Why doesn't GKN sponsor the project?

The curious thing about a letter like that is that once you have posted it you forget all about it with all the hurly-burly of office and project life. After all, it's all out of your hands once it's in the postbox.

I came back into the office on the Monday, rather late in the morning, to find the place buzzing with rumours.

People seemed to be avoiding me. There was an opened letter on my desk.

Dear Richard,

Thank you for your letter. I have been following the project with interest and I have spoken with your board. I think we should sponsor you — so please continue your work on the project full-time for the next 18 months and we will pay you. Please make sure that the GKN logo is positioned prominently on Thrust2. *Good luck.*

Yours sincerely,

Roy Roberts, Managing Director, GKN Group plc

I did my handovers, said my goodbyes and was gone within the hour.

Around this time I had a key meeting with the British Airways marketing team at their Cromwell Road headquarters in London. British Airways were getting very excited about the *Thrust2* prospects and their participation.

"We really should do this for British Airways — after all we have Concorde and we are the fastest airline in the world. But we haven't any money for you."

The meeting was about to terminate and fail when

one of the team came up with a completely off-the-wall promotional concept.

"Under international rules, we are allowed to refund used British Airways tickets. You supply us with used British Airways tickets and we will refund them."

This was an amazing opportunity to generate the Holy Grail of fund-raising — steady cashflow. I spent time with my friends involved in GKN overseas operations. They were unbelieving that we could fund the project from used BA tickets. Before long the programme started to build real mass and a very large number of executives on long-haul flights were choosing to fly British Airways and the used tickets were arriving in large numbers. By the time the first year was up and the contract was due for renewal, other companies were enquiring whether they could join the scheme.

We had a real winner on our hands, generating steady funding and 'scaleable'.

I turned up again at Cromwell Road for the contract-renewal meeting, which I was really looking forward to because we had done really well for them. There could now be a next and highly innovative stage in the relationship. But the meeting had been suddenly changed. I was not to meet the clever team who had put the original scheme together and I was ushered upstairs to meet the marketing manager. This might not be such a good omen. He had a very impressive large office with big windows and fitted out with black cork wall tiles and enlarged pictures of him shaking hands with famous classical orchestra conductors. It seemed a strange temple for a senior airline executive.

He opened the discussion.

"*Thrust2* is dangerous and we are a safe airline. Safety is everything, so I am now terminating our arrangement. We shouldn't be doing this."

I explained that the scheme had been very successful: the tickets were still flooding in from many sources and there were more applications from other companies wishing to join the scheme. I asked him what he was going to promote instead of *Thrust2*.

"British Airways is going to sponsor orchestras."

"You'll have to give me a couple of weeks, I said."

"Why's that, Richard? I have terminated our arrangement with immediate effect."

"It'll take me that time to get an orchestra together…"

But there wasn't much humour in the room that morning.

The 1980 stage of the programme was a tough exercise where reality would take over from the dream. It was July 1980 and the ex-RAF engine team of Tony Meston and Geoff Smee had the *Thrust2* car down on a test pan at RAF Coningsby and the engine running in full afterburner. The huge flame, noise and ground vibration reminded me of the ear-splitting Lightning demonstrations at Farnborough Air Shows. The next move was to drive the car and at last we had a venue: the Army School of Mechanical Transport had a driving school set up at the ex-RAF airfield at Leconfield in Yorkshire. Every other airfield had turned us down because of the huge engine noise — but Colonel Pat Reger had the right stuff.

"Of course, you have to come here — you can all live in the officers' mess."

To train army truck drivers, the huge runways had traffic lights and speed-limit reminders, which were confusing. And, even worse, a hump halfway down the runway meant that the far end was not visible.

At long last we were moving under our own power and Tony Meston was alongside on his motorcycle. We pulled up at the far end.

"How fast did you think you were going?" asked Tony with exasperation in his voice.

"About 80mph?" I ventured.

"You were doing 50mph!"

We had a very long way to go.

By the end of the Leconfield period we had reached 180mph with very cautious use of the afterburner. It wasn't a great start and the team had expected much better progress.

But after this we would be operating on the UK air show circuit on the best runways in the country, with the first runs at RNAS Lee-on-Solent on a brilliant flat runway.

Something clicked and we made a 200mph-plus run with full afterburner, brake parachute and huge noise. The crowds were highly appreciative.

After that it was a different air show every weekend, with more supporters and more experience every time.

It was time to try for the British Land Speed Record. The best runway in the country for this was at Greenham Common near Newbury, built for the United States Air Force base to US specifications. It was 10,000ft long. Curiously, we uncovered a Downing Street agreement with the US that allowed occasional use of the runway for British recreational purposes.

The record we really wanted was the flying mile and Dunlop had cleared our Lightning tyres to 260mph. We had to make two passes over the mile within the hour and that meant we started at one end aiming to be at 260mph on entry to the mile section, holding that speed for a nail-biting mile and then frantically braking at the far end. We were finishing up 12ft from the end of the runway using the big GQ parachute and brakes.

John was concerned by skid marks at the start of the *Thrust2* braking section that were affecting the car's stability in the crosswind conditions. We later discovered that the huge deceleration caused by the oversized brake parachute was causing the inertia of the heavy wheels to keep spinning forward even though the car was decelerating. The car accelerated like a bullet and we tried to hold 260mph for the mile, which was risky because the runway was only 1.9 miles long.

But now we had the team's first success and the British Land Speed Record for the mile at 247.87mph — which still stands.

The rest of the year was spent fitting the car with its beautiful aluminium bodywork — the work of Ron Benton, Gordy Flux, Mike Barrett, Brian Ball and many others at Ranelagh. Ron was an expert sheet-metal worker who had achieved an extraordinary career working on many famous British projects, a much-loved team member and a man of brilliant quotes: "Just give me more time and I'll finish it faster!"

So, 1981 was the year we were going to get the World

Land Speed Record. We needed over 629mph and we were full of confidence. We had been to 260mph. We were going to run on the hallowed salt at the Bonneville Salt Flats in Utah, USA. We had a brilliant team, an inexperienced driver and no money — what could possibly go wrong?

Plenty of ambition but no money...

And the first ever solid wheels. The car was going to travel so fast that special rubber tyres, if we could even get them, would be a huge risk because tyres could fail at 650mph speeds. We had to take the risk and develop solid aluminium High Duty Alloys wheels that would be safe but had never been tried before.

Michael Kemp, the well-known *Daily Mail* motoring correspondent, saved the day — and out of nowhere appeared Trust Securities, a property-development company with a new high-profile development at Heathrow. We had £25,000 and this was to turn into the most incredible story.

But first we had to finish the car. Our paint sponsors only had an overnight window in which to complete the paintwork. I was called at 1.00am the next morning.

"We can't finish the car and we'll have to stop."

"Why is that?"

"Ron Benton is still working on the other side of the

car and he is going to get painted in..."

Ron went home early that morning and on the way had a crash that could have killed him. He was driving his elderly Russian Moskvich van, which had become an extended toolbox and included several hundredweight of blacksmith's anvil loose in the back. Of all things Ron had to hit, it was a fire engine out on an emergency call going down Maidenhead High Street. The massive accident totalled the very solid Moskvich — but fortunately the flying anvil missed him.

Later we were all discussing the accident.

"How on earth did you hit a fire engine, Ron, with all the flashing lights and sirens?"

"I know — you still had your ear defenders on!"

Before we left for Bonneville, we managed to negotiate 'pluvius insurance', against rain falling at the desert, a deal at 75:1 for a £1,000 premium.

Once together on the famous Bonneville salt, our confidence failed big time. The car didn't appear to respond to its steering. Regardless of my efforts in the cockpit, it went sideways at 95mph.

All our learning on British runways was now of little value — this was absolutely different.

We tried again and went sideways and far into the desert at 175mph. The car was yawing around its rear-wheel axis and sooner or later it was going to go sideways and roll or fly — the typical Bonneville accident. At one stage the car went out of line and the experienced United States Auto Club officials were getting more and more concerned.

This was understandable because apparently the car was headed for their timing stand.

Each run was a disappointment, the track was getting rutted and I felt concerned about bringing in the afterburner and adding all that power to an unstable car on a track that looked increasingly like a railway line into Waterloo station.

I was playing it gently and not using full power.

This led to the team saying, 'Reheat is just a Myth'.

On one run I took John Ackroyd in the second seat to 400mph, a long-drawn-out, hazardous experience that John was never keen to repeat.

On October 10th we tried a two-run test with a turn-around between runs. This was a welcome alternative to the disappointing daily runs. We did the first run at 400mph and then the all-important one-hour turn-around procedure to prepare for the mandatory second run. It was a shambles — the tow truck broke its prop shaft, David Brinn, our accountant, found himself towing the car, and I was seriously angry at our chaotic failure. We restarted the car and, intent on getting some kind of record, I banged it into full reheat. Amazingly, the car went straight as a die and we were quickly up to over 440mph when the rough Bonneville ride resulted in loss of a battery connection, loss of fuel pressure, loss of power and loss of the recorder. The timekeepers gave us an average of 447mph for the two runs, which suggests that the car peaked at around 475mph or more — we were the fastest-ever British car.

We could do it. We knew how to drive the car: accelerate and decelerate as hard as possible and don't try to cruise it!

But it wasn't to be. That night there was a fearsome storm on the desert and we hung on tight to the camp tents, which were secured to the car. The next morning the Bonneville flats were flooded for the winter. We had to go home just at the point when we thought we had the record cracked.

Of course, there was no money. The car had to go to a German motor show to get some revenue into the system and we had to get the project back on the rails. Of course, we were seen as a failure and my job was to get the funds flowing again. The BBC helpfully screened a documentary about the attempt showing everyone sloshing about in the Bonneville floods.

Of course... the answer lay with the insurance pay-out at 75:1! I contacted the insurance company who duly responded by explaining that they were appointing an assessor.

"Who pays the assessor?" I asked.

"We do," they said — which opened up a new range of concerns.

The assessor duly decided there was no claim because there was no record attempt. We explained that the whole event was a record attempt: there were official timekeepers on site and we had cracked the driving procedure and were on our way — until it rained. There was stalemate.

GKN House in Kingsway, Holborn, London was the location for the sponsors' meeting. The long-faced sponsors sat around the table and it seemed like a wake. Everyone was focused on the director of the insurance company — were they going to pay? Then we had a truly fabulous moment.

I announced that we had invited the media for a press announcement in 10 days' time and there appeared to be a good response — the media were now following us.

"Why wasn't I told of this?" the insurance director asked.

We explained that it was a sponsors' event and

insurance was a cost centre.

"What are you going to say about the insurance?" the director asked.

"Simple. It's your decision. If you decide to pay, we'll praise you to the skies. If you decide not to pay, we'll terminate the project and circulate your policy to the media.

"You wouldn't do that," was the director's angry response.

"Please understand, we have to."

On the day a large media posse turned up to the London press meeting and we had absolutely no idea how it would go...

The director showed up with a smile on his face and a cheque for £75,000 in a beautiful light grey leather wallet. The project would continue.

But the most amazing story of all came from the generous people at Trust Securities. They had got themselves into a bit of major bother on a new site in Manchester where the only site access could be obtained by purchasing the home of a local resident who had told everyone he had absolutely no intention of selling. Full of concern, the Trust directors rang his doorbell.

"Who are you?" they were asked.

"We are directors of Trust Securities."

"Were you anything to do with the Project Thrust Land Speed Record?"

"Well, er, yes… we were sponsors."

"Well, come right in and let's talk…"

By sheer good fortune the homeowner was a *Thrust* enthusiast. Trust Securities explained that in grateful return for recovery from a very expensive disaster they would help sponsor the project to its conclusion.

Of course, 1982 was going to be the record year. Hadn't we been to nearly 500mph. Hadn't we learned all the lessons?

The answer was that we hadn't — and we were still just raw beginners.

But there was to be a brilliant experience. *Thrust2* had been designed by John to do demonstration runs on race circuits — just in case we had the opportunity. The *Daily Express* were holding their Tourist Trophy meeting at Silverstone. With the intention of shaking up the well-financed circuit racing community, we towed *Thrust2* out to the track and positioned it for a start in front of the stands crammed with enthusiasts. We started her up and I did a full reheat start down the track with all 17,000lbs of thrust. The effect was spectacular: mechanics were all standing on the pit wall and their usual motor racing ear defenders were hopeless against the huge noise of the reheated Avon, a more powerful 302 version now. I saw them clutching their ears in pain as we accelerated past at over 120mph.

Somehow we made it around Copse corner and then I taxied around the circuit, returning to the grandstands and, of all things, a standing ovation from the crowd. But the best bit was yet to come.

We put *Thrust2* on display behind the stands and we were submerged with a huge crowd of excited racegoers. The Silverstone policeman was there.

"Do you know, Richard, I have been attending Silverstone racing for 25 years and I have never seen anything like your display. It made my helmet shake!"

June 16th, 1982 was a truly terrible day. *Thrust2* had been carefully rebuilt after all the ravages of the Bonneville salt and we were back at Greenham Common doing tests and performing 260mph runs for a sponsors' day. The weather and the setting were absolutely perfect. I had spent the morning collecting parachutes from Irvin in Essex and, to save our high-speed chutes from wear on the runway, we were using ex-military aircraft braking chutes.

We had just made the last run and John Ackroyd had cleared the car for transit to Bonneville. The sun was low in the day and I asked everyone for one more run since I was short of 1982 experience. All agreed to a repeat of the earlier run plan. Mike Barrett was to travel in the passenger seat. The peak speed was to be no more than 230mph and the Jaguar fire tender saloon was to be positioned by the runway as a reminder point to cut the power and deploy the brake parachute.

We set off in full afterburner and then something happened that I cannot explain. Somehow I missed the Jaguar and accelerated for too long. There was smoke from the front tyres, which had expanded with the speed and were fouling the bodywork. *Thrust2* reached 300mph and I deployed the military chute — which promptly failed. I thought I had shut down the engine but it seems that I had only got down to idle power. Our only means of braking was now the wheel brakes and I applied them hard — so hard that we had 4,000ft of skid marks. We were now down to 180mph and to avoid crashing through the boundary hedge and into the local quarry, I turned us left for the perimeter track and put us onto the rough grass. Mike was OK but the car was badly damaged. We removed the remains to a nearby hangar and the team went into deep shock. One moment we were ready to go to the US, the next we had wrecked our car and our chances.

There were three problems: the car was badly damaged at the front; the engine had ingested damaging debris; and my credibility as the driver was blown. John Ackroyd was mortified. As a team we all pulled together — and as penance and proof of ability I had to get my IMC pilot's instrument rating in three weeks while Mike Barrett led the team through the rebuild at Ranelagh. But then there was the question of the precious and wrecked Avon 302 engine.

Nobody wanted to help. We had changed from great British hopefuls to wasteful and incompetent pariahs. We had been given a chance and we had blown it. Rolls-Royce wanted £80,000 to rebuild the engine — and there were no other Avon 302s available. The entire project was ruined.

Then the phone rang. It was John Watkins, head of the engine bay at RAF Binbrook in Lincolnshire, home of the last Lightning squadrons.

"We would like to see the engine, please. We have never known one so badly damaged."

It would cost us £200 to get the engine to Binbrook, but this was not the time to lose any remaining friends. The engine went up to Binbrook.

The hunt for a replacement engine went on. There was one unit that had been used for testbed work but no one had any idea of its condition. Meanwhile the Ranelagh team went on with the major strip-down and rebuild of the car.

I was tearing my hair out, angry at having spoiled the team's and sponsors' chances and years of their work with one second of stupid personal error.

Then the phone rang. It was John Watkins again with a call I'll never ever forget.

"Richard, we have looked at the engine and it's badly damaged. What do you want us to do with it now?"

"John, we have no money and with the engine ruined, I can't spend money recovering it. Can you please dump it wherever you dump the RAF scrap. I am trying to locate a replacement but I am not having much luck."

John's tone changed dramatically.

"Richard, now why would you want to do that, when the Binbrook engine-bay team has worked nights in their own time rebuilding the engine and the Queen has paid for the parts?"

It was a truly incredible situation. Thanks to sponsors, the Royal Air Force and the *Thrust* team, we were going to survive and continue. We still haven't discovered the engine-bay messages recorded deep in the engine guts!

Einstein had it right. His definition of insanity: doing

the same thing over and over again and expecting different results.

We were going back to Bonneville in 1982, this time with wider front wheels. There was another important difference: Ken Norris had agreed to manage the team on the desert and his quiet authority held the organisation together in a brilliant and friendly way.

This time we were organised, the sponsors had taken out the desert insurance, and we thought we knew what we were doing. We had a high level of confidence. All we needed was another 150mph.

The very day we arrived at the Bonneville town of Wendover, the rain returned in a fury and Bonneville Salt Flats was suddenly a lake. But there was no way we could go back home without running the car. Something had to happen.

John believed that the answer lay at Alvord Lake in Oregon and immediately set off with my brother Charles to check it out. At this point Peter Moore, fanatical private flyer and accountant (in that order), arrived on the scene and suggested the Black Rock. He and I piled into his Subaru and set off for Gerlach, Nevada, travelling overland via Winnemucca. The Black Rock Desert was incredible: 140 square miles of absolutely flat desert and the surface was dried, hard, brown mud with a bit of give. It promised to be slightly softer than the hard salt at Bonneville and there was accommodation in the small town of Gerlach.

Of course, there were problems but given the fact we were late in the year, the Bureau of Land Management (BLM) agreed to allow immediate slow-speed testing. At 400mph the car felt in its element. The runs were smooth and the steering worked well with the new front wheels.

John reported that the car was actually working harder when on the road transport trailer than on the ground. It was all looking good.

And that was the moment the short-term licence was pulled.

The Nevada Outdoor Recreation Association, dedicated to environmental concerns, had taken exception both to the British impudence of somehow getting permission to trial on the desert and also the possibility of the desert surface being damaged. The immediate response from the citizens of Gerlach and Empire was nothing short of incredible. Within 24 hours they had 600 signatures on their appeal and presented it on television to Susan Lynn for Congressman Jim Santini.

The next day the licence was restored and Susan

Lynn said, "As far as I am concerned, these guys are honourable people working very hard to anticipate the BLM's requirements. They're honest, first-class people."

Thrust2 was operational again. But the odds were against a record in 1982: the temperature was dropping, there was rain, the course was soggy in places. The best the team could manage was a 590mph average but the instruments suggested *Thrust2* had peaked at 615mph.

It was time to go home and recuperate — it had been an incredibly difficult year for everyone.

Of course, 1983 *had* to be the year. We had the car, the desert, the sponsors — and we needed just 50mph. But that's 50mph in the transonic speed range where the car was beginning to create huge power-sapping shock waves.

The big question was whether the Avon 302 engine had enough power for the job.

The question seemed settled on the seventh run when, in front of the then record holder Gary Gabelich, *Thrust2* could only manage 607mph.

"Nice run, nice run!" said Gabelich, sure in the belief that his record for the mile, 622.407mph, was safe for many years to come.

Privately we believed the engine had surged and

was probably seriously damaged.

John Watkins appeared from the UK just in time to join George Webb, the Avon engine specialist kindly sent by the Rolls-Royce main board. The engine was all right; it needed adjustment and the afterburner control linkage had not been correctly set. George ran a compressor wash to clean the engine through and we were ready to go again. We now had much more power.

John Ackroyd changed the run timings. Previously we had run in the early mornings when visibility was at its best, but then the temperature was low and this dragged down the speed of sound and the onset of the huge transonic aero drag. From now on we would run at the hottest part of the day when the local speed of sound was at its highest and therefore the transonic drag threshold was at a higher speed for the car.

On October 4th we finally got the world record for the mile at 633.468mph, with the fastest run from the south 'hard' end of the course being 642.971mph for the mile. But the magic number was the peak speed of 650.88mph: we had got our extra 50mph and, even better, the car had achieved its design speed. It was a huge credit to John and the engineering team.

We Brits and our American friends sat down for a raucous dinner that night, celebrating in grand style an achievement that would change all our lives.

The Queen sent us a fax of congratulations from Buckingham Palace — which impressed the Americans no end. They stood up and made a speech and toasted the Queen of England.

I had to reply.

"I'd like everyone to raise their glasses and toast President Reagan of the United States."

This didn't go down at all well.

"Richard," said the Americans, "if you don't mind we'll stick with your Queen!"

Once back in UK, I was invited to a wash-up meeting with the Initial Services board. They were very pleased with the joint achievement and there was an incredible surprise in store. It seems that the sponsorship had so motivated the entire company that the financial benefits had appeared in the annual accounts. The board explained that they had not been expecting this and it came as a most welcome surprise. As no systems had been put in place to identify and directly measure these benefits, the collective view was that they had accrued directly from participating in the *Thrust2* programme.

It had taken nine years to bring the world record back to Britain — and now it was time to move on.

CHAPTER 3
ARV SUPER2

"Well, Ron, are we going to certificate?"

Chairman, Civil Aviation Authority

Bruce Giddings, a clever and original designer with a very sharp wit, was lucky to be alive. It was 1983 and the big breakthrough in aviation was the development of the microlight. The Americans had developed the Rogallo sail-like wing for spaceshot recovery and military use, and the development of high-powered, lightweight, two-stroke engines made it possible to combine the two and have your own go-anywhere low-cost aircraft, without the inconvenience of a pilot's licence and associated bureaucracy.

With no regulation in place, there was a global rash of new designs and even more dangerous own designs. The accident rate was appalling and it was said that some 60 would-be pilots had already been killed in France. Bruce had designed and built his own microlight and taught himself to fly and was keen to avoid the dead hand of regulation from the British Civil Aviation Authority, which seemed to be undecided about this new, fast-growing sport and extraordinarily remote from it.

I had qualified to fly light aircraft as part of my training for *Thrust2* and I loved the sport and the personal satisfaction. Every flight was different and required varied skills regardless of whether you were covering the same track as before. But there was a problem: it was far too expensive and I discussed all this with Ken Norris, designer of Donald Campbell's *Bluebird*, at his flying club in Bournemouth. They weren't making huge money, it was just the cost of keeping the old museum pieces in the air. Good examples were the Cessna 150 and later 152 types, which were good, solid, basic trainers, but their designs dated from the 1950s and their engines from the 1930s. There were over 30,000 of these aircraft built and if the operating cost could be brought down with better products, there could be a massive replacement market.

If the World Land Speed Record could be achieved with a small company on a minute budget, what else could such a team achieve?

Bruce introduced me to Nick Sibley and James Morton, who had been building the Sheriff light twin aircraft at Sandown airport. The project had run out of money and the Sheriff was stillborn. We formed a team and headed down the route of designing a Cessna replacement.

The outline design came together very quickly. An aeroplane with its single engine at the front has to balance about a third of the width of the wing. Since the engine is the heaviest part of the airframe and is positioned right at the front, it defines the size and weight of the entire two-seater aircraft. If the engine could be much lighter, the plane could be made smaller to do the same job. Not only that, but the smaller aircraft should be cheaper to build and burn less fuel as there was less of an aircraft to drag through the sky.

The wing, of course, provides the lift to keep the aircraft in the sky but the wing only carries the load if the aircraft is moving fast enough. If it slows up, the aircraft stalls and drops out of the sky. Towards each end of the wing are the control surfaces known as the ailerons, which are effectively plates that work in opposition to each other and enable the pilot to control the aircraft in roll. But there is a classic problem: if the pilot lets the aircraft fly too slowly, the airflow breaks down over the wing ends and we have a stall; the flow breaks down first at the wing tips and over the ailerons, and with turbulent flow over their surfaces the ailerons will no longer work and the pilot has no roll control left. This can lead to the dreaded stall/spin accident, which often may not be survivable.

Bruce, Nick and James decided to employ a smart solution: sweep the wings forward by just four degrees. Then, at the stall, the airflow breaks down at the wing root, where it joins the body of the aircraft, and the ailerons remain effective in smooth air at all times.

Bruce also had a particular interest in making the forward fuselage or body of the plane out of superplastic aluminium to provide great strength and protect the occupants. Superplastic aluminium is a method of forming large aluminium panels using heat and suction to pull the aluminium sheet into a large female mould — the metallic equivalent of forming a plastic domestic bath. These large panels would enable the aircraft to have a beautiful, distinctive, rounded shape.

The company was named ARV Aviation, ARV standing for Air Recreational Vehicle, an American acronym that appeared to have currency for the new generation of light aircraft. Our aircraft was to be called the Super2, standing for superplastic aluminium, two seats and the two-stroke engine.

In France they realised they had the same problem: the old Cessna and Piper aircraft were expensive to operate and this was made worse by adverse exchange rates. The French government realised that action was needed and set up a design competition, the idea being that the winner would receive a substantial government-funded order for some 60 copies of this primary training aeroplane. The competition winner was the Robin aircraft company in Dijon.

This was one of the times that I wished I lived in so sensible and practical France.

Back on our side of the Channel, the key bogey in all this was the aircraft certification. By law, we would be unable to sell production versions unless the aircraft was certificated, and the certification would have to be cleared by Britain's Civil Aviation Authority, an august body that did not appear to certificate many light aircraft. To satisfy everyone, the CAA would also have to certify the design and build organisation, which would control quality but also massively increase start-up cost. An extended certification procedure or failure to certify at all would have an expensive impact on the brave shareholders who were prepared to join us in the battle to change light aviation.

But the potential was tremendous — a global market of some 20,000 units.

Having a rather jaundiced outlook on British administrative bodies, I went straight to the CAA to open the discussions. The two certification standards were BCAR Section K for the airframe and BCAR Section S for the engine.

"If we meet both BCAR Section K and BCAR Section S, will you certify the aircraft to transport category?"

They said they would. This was an easy statement for them because meeting the conditions was a seriously tough call both in engineering and financial terms. Many projects had not lasted the course.

"Look, I have to deal with city bankers and investors. They don't understand aeroplanes and they have to know that we have a chance of getting this through. So can you please give me that statement in writing."

They agreed — and this turned out to be our key to survival.

With help from my cousin Jamie, a major city bank decided to take a chance on us. Not only did they invest but also many of the senior executives joined in to take advantage of government tax breaks.

So the money started to flow and Bruce, Nick and James began to move the programme forward. More investors joined and the programme grew in confidence. But there was still a major problem: we were missing an engine.

The best place to start was Champion, a *Thrust2* sponsor.

"You do spark plugs — who is developing a lightweight aero engine?"

Champion made enquiries and came back with Lotus and Hewland.

The Lotus engine looked the most likely. It was a really beautiful, horizontally opposed, four-stroke, four-cylinder engine, but it had yet to run and there were most probably many months of development ahead.

Bruce and Nick went to Hewland, manufacturer of racing gearboxes in Maidenhead, and came back with an amazing story. Mike Hewland had developed the Hewland Arrow engine for his son's go-kart racing career and then extended it into a two-cylinder engine for the microlight market. The engine was mature and flying — Mike and Bruce came back with an example. This had to be the way forward.

Months later back at ARV's Sandown airport design base, I was greeted with long faces.

"The calculations don't work — 55 horsepower isn't

enough. The aircraft will need a Heathrow-like long runway to get airborne."

The next day I was with Mike Hewland at the Maidenhead factory.

"Mike, we need more horsepower."

"How much?"

"Ideally 75."

"OK, I'll add another cylinder…"

And that was that. The amazing capability of Hewland's gearbox and powertrain business meant that the three-cylinder engine was up and running within a month.

Mike was always a man of few words. His engine made 75bhp first pop on the dyno — smooth as silk! It is most unusual for this to happen.

I was in big trouble on March 11th, 1985. It was my wife Sally's birthday and it was also the first flight of the Super2 — an amazing 13 months from start with no money, no team, no engine. Nick was really pleased because he had had regular visits from Hugh Kendall, the wartime test pilot from Miles Aircraft and well-known air racer. Hugh was semi-retired and also lived on the Isle of Wight.

Hugh was another man of very few words but they were worth listening to.

"I am going to do your test flying!"

We all lined up on the west side of the Sandown grass runway. Hugh made a number of trial high-speed runs with ARV 001 to satisfy himself that all was in order and then he went for it. We all thought it was just another test run, but then it became clear that the engine was flat out and the aircraft had to fly — there was no runway stopping distance left. He lifted off smoothly and headed north, flying a very high circuit. We all cheered — and then it struck us all that we had to get Hugh down again in safety. We watched him travel downwind to the south, make a left turn to base and then line up for his final approach.

Then the engine stopped. The propeller was stationary and we all gasped — there was nothing we could do.

But Hugh, the ace pilot, glided the aircraft in on its first landing and rolled to a halt at the midpoint of the runway. The engine had stopped because of a carburation problem and Hugh had suffered exhaust fumes in the cockpit, but he said the aircraft handled really well.

Of course, the project was always finance-critical, but at least our plane flew. At around this time we approached the Department of Trade & Industry with a request to participate in a very smart scheme. They would be prepared to buy three copies of a new product and put it into the marketplace to test acceptance and give the manufacturers valuable feedback. We really needed that deal and I had several meetings with the DTI people in London. The ARV team were very negative about this.

"The DTI only give money to large companies like Rolls-Royce where there's seen to be minimal risk — it's a waste of time."

I persevered. After all, there was a deal to be had, but when I was asked to complete a book-sized application form, I gave up. It was going to take far too long to get them their data and it was explained that it would take some months to make the decision. They couldn't tell me whether they had the finance to fund the aircraft purchase.

After the first flight, I tried once again — and I met with the same DTI inspector. But this time I had the video of the first flight to show.

"Is this the same aeroplane?" he asked, dumbfounded.

"Yes, it's the ARV Super2 on its first flight."

"I can't believe you have achieved this so quickly…"

"Well, we did. New design, new airframe, new engine and first flight, all in 13 months from no-funds start."

For some reason, probably us, the inspector explained that the DTI trial product offer was now closed and so there was no reason to continue.

Many years later I was able to take him for a flight in a Super2 and he went away very deep in thought.

As Chief Engineer, Nick was now leading the team into the certification phase — every part of the aircraft had to be approved. Bruce was towing a trailer fitted with ARV wheels and tyres for umpteen miles on the Isle of Wight roads — there were expensive structural tests as parts of the aircraft were 'Loaded to Proof'. James had set up an engine test shed at the northern end of the airfield, running the Hewland test engine day and night.

The programme started well enough with a huge aviation menu known as the Compliance Checklist. The idea was that the CAA specialist surveyors would make their inspection visits and when satisfied with a component would sign it off. Once all the checks on the checklist were signed off, we should be certificated. The CAA sent in bills for fees and expenses with every visit. It was time-consuming and very expensive.

About this time I made my first flight in a Super2. I loaded the plane with maximum fuel and set off for an extended trip around the Isle of Wight. It was a beautiful day. When I landed, Hugh was upset.

"You were only supposed to fly a circuit — we thought you had lost it somewhere."

Shortly after, and back at our new sales office at Blackbushe airport, Nick phoned.

"Richard, it's not working. The CAA surveyors are not signing off on the checklist. We will go bust if it goes on like this. We have to pay but they are not delivering."

"Nick, surely at least one surveyor has signed something somewhere?"

"No — they're not signing."

I went to the CAA in Redhill and it was clear that there was a serious problem. The surveyors had been involved with other light-aircraft projects and seen them go bust before certification, so they assumed that ARV, being a highly innovative design with insecure funding, would not last the course.

When they realised that there was a major city bank behind the programme, the certification gathered pace and they started signing.

But even so the certification process was taking forever. Whilst all our work had been done, the aircraft still was not certificated and we were unable to fund up for production. By now, with three ARVs flying, we had 200 sales enquiries from all over the world — but no certification.

Extreme measures were needed. It appeared that despite the CAA's letter of confidence, they were not going to deliver and our shareholders would lose their funds.

I managed to get past the CAA Chairman's dragon-like secretarial gate guardian on the phone and found myself talking with him. This had to be very quick before he put the phone down.

"What do you want?" he said.

"We are your smallest customer I'm here to bring you good news — and the CAA never seems to get in the news unless something has crashed and that's bad for everyone."

He was still listening.

"Working with the CAA at Redhill, we are about to certificate a new all-British training and leisure aircraft and we have 200 sales enquiries. It's the start of a completely new city-financed industry and the CAA ought to be ready for the public interest and the story. May I come and brief you?"

"Yes," he said. "My secretary will fix it."

The meeting was to take place and I was fed up with the bankers' continual demand for finalisation of the certification process — a process over which none of us at ARV had any further control. So I invited them to join the meeting so they could witness all this for themselves.

As a group we were invited into the CAA Chairman's office — everything, but everything, was on the line. Frustrated certification probably meant the end of the project. I introduced everyone and handed the Chairman an ARV model for his desk while tea was poured. Before I could go any further, the bankers waded in and took control.

"Mr Chairman, are you ever going to certificate this aeroplane?"

I was horrified. It was so blatant and aggressive — and we were dealing with an organisation with absolute authority. Upset the Chairman and everything could be lost.

The Chairman, of course, was used to this aggression and turned to the Head of Airworthiness sitting on his left. All this was now completely out of my control.

"Well, Ron," he said. "Are we going to certificate?"

"There are one or two points we're not happy with," replied Ron, "but it's a very good aeroplane and a great effort from such a small and impressive start-up team. Yes, we are going to certificate."

The emotion in the room was extraordinary. Collectively, the ARV team had passed one of the most difficult exams imaginable.

The bankers immediately made their apologies and left me with the Chairman and Head of Airworthiness to finish our teas and talk aeroplanes. The Sandown team were over the moon — it really was a huge team achievement.

Now we had to build aeroplanes and sell them. The Chairman entered into the spirit of the achievement and we flew three ARVs into Heathrow to announce our certification and receive our Type Certificate. When British Airways realised that the CAA Chairman was on site, they quickly wheeled up a Concorde and the pictures were taken as the all-important certificate was handed over.

Then the fun started. We had to get out of Heathrow and it was peak traffic time. The three little ARVs left the engineering base like a string of ducklings and proceeded along the taxiways. I now realised how really dangerous this was — the light aircraft were incredibly vulnerable from airliner jet blast and passengers in the huge airliners were crammed at the windows watching the progress of these three tiny aircraft with incredulity.

"Golf Delta Echo Xray Papa — cleared take-off,

runway 27 left, left-hand turnout."

We hared down the huge runway and as soon as I was airborne I made a sharp left turn and headed south at low level for our sales office at Blackbushe. We were safe.

The money had come and now we were into production — again an incredibly difficult programme for a small team starting from scratch. An aeroplane, like most things, is simply a collection of parts and the labour required to put it all together. The parts have to be made at the best prices and the labour content is controlled by the tooling investment and the dreaded learning curve. The tooling relates to the temporary jigs needed to hold the parts together while the labour is used to fix them. Every tooling investment decision has to be made in the context of the amount of labour the tooling will save and the number of aircraft to be built. In view of the huge market interest, we bravely decided we were going for continuous production, which put huge pressure on the sales team to deliver a constant stream of orders.

And then there is the dreaded learning curve. At the start of the programme a brave decision is made defining the 'fully learned hours' needed to build the aeroplane. This assumes that the entire aircraft construction process has progressed to a point where the aircraft build is 'fully learned'. But the first aircraft are incredibly expensive because the build team is learning how to assemble them. After that it gets progressively easier as the job is mastered and more short cuts and improvements are made. But major changes on the aircraft are incredibly expensive because the specification has been certificated and set in stone. We took advice and worked to an 85 per cent learning curve that would eventually get us to a fully learned and profitable position by aircraft number 100. Before number 100, the aircraft would be more expensive to make because of the increased labour cost and that has a huge effect on the business plan. Those early aircraft are more expensive to make than they can be sold for and gradually the manufacturing cost is worked down until number 100, when the full sales margin is made and trading profits are made. This means that the capital investment must cover the cost of the learning curve — and that was really painful because the capital investment was an unprofessional negotiation with the banks who pushed and expected to see every aircraft sold with every extra included and a very considerable return on the investment. The business plan they chose to invest in was highly ambitious and almost unachievable

— but this was clearly the only way forward.

There is a long history of aircraft manufacture on the Isle of Wight and the ARV build team was exceptional. There was a general feel about the programme that it was a winner and would provide the teams with continuous and valuable employment in the long term. They just had to work hard at the early stages to get the quality and numbers right.

With over 100 people working, very soon we saw a new aircraft delivered every week and the quality improving with each one. The new owners would come to the island to collect their planes and once back home the flying clubs would swing into action to use them.

This then led to an extraordinary situation. At Blackbushe the sales team had three aircraft that were used for demonstration flights at flying clubs and for sales prospects visiting Blackbushe. The problem was that the aircraft were proving popular at the flying clubs and were building hours quickly.

We needed to be ahead in the hours race with our aircraft so we could encounter engineering problems first, before the operational fleet. This meant we had to arrive at the office early, fly before office hours, then again at lunchtime and, if daylight permitted, again in the evening. It was a race to build flying hours, but one that in all probability we could never win.

At this stage in the story the most amazing event happened. The bankers had decided that because they were making their investment decisions on a traditional basis they were getting poor results and now they were prepared to consider original thinking. They would invest in the entrepreneur instead of their traditional approach, which was their assessment of the product. To do this they would need to study their investee entrepreneurs.

To do this we were invited to a hotel near Staines in Middlesex. The idea was that the group were to spend Saturday in individual meetings with an industrial psychologist who, together with his team, would put together the assessments overnight. There was to be a wash-up meeting on the Sunday morning.

I couldn't spare the working Saturday but turned up on the Sunday morning for breakfast and the wash-up. I realised I was working with a completely different outlook to the other entrepreneurs as I parked my MG Montego Turbo alongside the rows of Porsches. Inside was a classic collection of entrepreneurs who explained that as the drinks had been on the bank, they had just had the most alcoholic evening any of them could remember.

We all sat down to breakfast facing a clear section of the room where there were two flip charts, each with a very elegant and expensive grey leather cover. Also fussing around the flip charts was clearly the industrial psychologist — who looked extremely uncomfortable. This was going to be interesting. The senior banker brought the meeting to order.

"As you know, we wanted to learn more about the characteristics of our entrepreneurs and you very kindly agreed to be interviewed. We decided to use the bank staff as a control. I will be the first to admit this didn't work out as planned."

At this point he handed over to the psychologist, who took a deep breath and went over to the flip charts.

Flipping the cover of the first chart, he announced his findings of entrepreneurs' characteristics: very cautious, careful, committed team players driven by careful analysis and by their heads, and very risk-adverse.

He then went to the bankers' flip chart: wild, emotionally ego-driven executives, most akin to gamblers.

"Can anyone explain this?"

I put my hand up.

"When we come to the bank for a refinance, we bring the team — chief engineer, financial director and others — and we present to just one member of the bank's staff. That person can't possibly be an expert in all subjects, so there has to be an element of gambling."

We never discovered the eventual outcome of the event — but it was a truly memorable and very brave experience!

Seeing that as a team we were struggling with the huge workload and lack of experience, the bankers suggested politely that we needed experienced help. The CEO who was appointed had a background in big aircraft manufacture, which was just what we thought we all needed and welcomed, but very soon he was persuading the bankers that a different engine was needed — and any major change is a massive cost. Certainly more power would improve the aircraft, but a new uncertificated engine would require very considerable development and the aircraft would have to be recertificated. This was costing money that was urgently needed for production.

At about this time I drove around Europe meeting flying clubs and manufacturers. They seemed to understand the situation but with the exceptions of Italy and France no one seemed to be doing anything about it. On the way down through France I dropped in unannounced on the Robin factory in Dijon. The

Maestro, Pierre Robin, was not amused — what was this *rosbif* doing in his factory? I gave him an invitation to come and spend time with us in Sandown and fly the ARV but he was non-committal. But his sales director got the message and I had a factory tour and then an opportunity to fly the Robin ATL, which gave the impression of being a delicate and well-behaved first trainer but very different to the extrovert ARV, which you could throw around the sky like a small fighter.

Unlike the hopeless British government, the French government was incredibly supportive and really got behind the project, resulting in the first batch of 30 aircraft sales, a huge and valuable commitment that helped Robin production to work its way along the dreaded learning curve, and total ATL production reached over 130. But in Britain our sales were very hard-won with zero government support. The attitude was traditionally British negative, with flying clubs stating that they would wait until we became successful and well established. The DTI support would have been most welcome at this critical time — but it was not to be. We were to learn the hard lesson: never expect much in the way of government support or even commitment.

ARV did really well until we had the most unexpected engine problems. A student pilot at Shoreham airport started up his ARV and was surprised to find that the engine worked but the propeller didn't go round — clearly there was a problem and he wasn't going flying. It seemed that a seal in the Hewland engine had come loose, resulting in the engine running very slowly at idle, and at this low speed the propeller shaft couldn't take the low-frequency, high-torque firing hits from the engine cylinders and sheared.

We raced around the country replacing engine gearboxes but eventually the problem was beyond us and the aircraft had to be grounded by us and the CAA, and the workforce laid off. The sales team were close to landing a multi-aircraft deal in Essex and had to come home and leave the demonstration aircraft behind.

A few days later we sat around the table with the bankers. We examined the engineering problem, which could easily be solved, but the bankers were tired of ARV and the fight to create an aircraft industry — and, just like the early *Thrust2* sponsors, they left the table one by one. ARV was over. How could this happen to a certificated aircraft with a potential market of 20,000? To me it just meant that the project became a lot tougher and the bankers had failed the test. I delivered an aircraft to Liverpool and went home.

ARV Aviation went into administration and the next

phase of its tortured life.

Many years later I was able to buy ARV number 12 and renew my licence. After a few years we had a major problem that related to an uplift of contaminated fuel and coincided with an inexplicable engine problem. We took the aircraft to my home, took the fuselage apart to release and clean the tank, and finally sorted the engine problem, which was due to corrosion in the exhaust system. I was lucky enough to do the subsequent flight test with Paul Mulcahy, the CAA's chief test pilot who every week flew a wide range of aircraft from business jets to light aircraft. As we returned to land at Farnborough, he turned to me.

"You know, Richard, it's very rare to find a light aircraft that handles as well as this. It must have been a really great team that created it."

On July 15th, 2006, my ARV G-BMWE completed its 1,000th flight.

But my ARV story doesn't end there. In August 2006 I was lecturing in Manchester and the next day headed south to Popham airfield, near Basingstoke. It was a pleasant day with high cloud and after escaping Manchester's dangerous low-level transit alley I decided to land at Tatenhill at Burton-upon-Trent to top up the fuel and grab a sandwich. I continued south, enjoying the aircraft and weather, and then suddenly there was a smell of burning rubber. With hundreds of hours on ARVs I had never had that smell before.

I glanced at the coolant temperature gauge and saw the needle swing across the arc. The engine was going to be out of coolant soon and I was going to crash. The coolant pump had failed.

I called Coventry radar and asked their advice. They suggested going into Birmingham but flying over all those houses with a dying engine and disrupting a major international airport was a non-starter.

I called Tatenhill, explained the situation and told them I was coming back on a reciprocal course. I asked them to clear the circuit but with a failing engine I might not make it.

On the way back the engine began to break up and I shut it down. If the engine breaks up and falls out of the plane, the resulting out-of-balance crash might not be survivable — and I was enjoying a really lovely peaceful glide! I called the Tatenhill tower and explained that I wasn't going to make it.

"Good luck, Richard," they responded. It was a bit like a movie — but this was desperately serious and for real.

And then, there in front of me, was the perfect forced-landing site — a huge field freshly harrowed. This was brilliant: the set piece for the safest and absolute textbook forced landing. But it wasn't to be...

I was too high to start the approach so I made a couple of spiral turns to lose height and set up the approach into the wind, but with full flaps the aircraft wouldn't maintain air speed, so I had to come in steeply like the Space Shuttle and the risk was now to flare either too early and pancake in from 20ft or flare too late and crash nose first at some 60mph. I got it wrong and the aircraft went in nose first and somersaulted violently on its back. The destruction was extraordinary — everything was broken. The battery, for instance, broke its mountings and catapulted though the aluminium upper fuselage as if it was paper and landed some 20ft away. The altimeter adjustment knob made a hole in my forehead — but I was out through a small hole in the wrecked canopy in seconds.

Thank you, Bruce Giddings, James Morton and Nick Sibley — your decision to use superplastic aluminium for the fuselage all those years ago saved my life!

CHAPTER 4
CONCORDE

"British Airways wants to celebrate
10 years of safe Concorde operation into
New York and we have decided to set
a record. Would you be interested?"
Concorde Promotions Office, British Airways

The phone rang in the ARV Blackbushe office. Hopefully this was another Super2 sales prospect — but it wasn't. This time it was about a bigger and much faster bird.

The voice at the other end explained that he was from the Concorde Promotions Office. They were coming up to the 10th anniversary of the first commercial Concorde flight into Kennedy New York and wanted to set some sort of a transatlantic record. They had invited various television personalities but they were all too expensive. I got the impression they were scraping the barrel when it came to me.

"I'll do it for nothing!"

This led to the most unreal experience. They planned

to celebrate by flying the very same Concorde into Kennedy crewed by the very same crew and with a collection of VIPs, journalists and British Airways directors aboard. Once at Kennedy they wanted me to dash out of the plane first and then race through the boarding tunnels and board the Concorde in the next bay to head back to Heathrow immediately. Once back at Heathrow, I would join the next Concorde with minutes to spare and fly back to New York.

They reckoned that if it were done smartly, the whole experience involving no fewer than three transatlantic flights could be done in 12 hours. This wasn't exactly the life-and-death, high-risk achievement of a real aviation pioneer like Charles Lindbergh. But it would be an interesting personal experience.

We ran into immediate difficulties with US immigration, who would not let me cross from one Concorde to the next without passing through immigration. As we all know, US immigration can involve substantial delays and we were running against the clock. The immigration people demanded my personal presence to check my identity against my appalling passport mugshot. The solution was easy — fly out the weekend before for a dry run. Amazingly, the US authorities agreed to this.

So, over the prior weekend, I went to New York and back on Concorde. The US authorities were very helpful once they realised I had no record of moral turpitude: they would set up a special desk in the departure lounge and would stamp my passport on the run.

Concorde close-up is the most beautiful bird. I used to live in Twickenham and when the plane was flying from the easterly runway it would turn above Teddington with a thunderous roar and pedestrians would stop in their tracks and look up in awe at what the English and French had achieved as another load of 100 passengers headed off for New York and expected to be there in just three and a half hours. At air shows we would marvel at the sheer beauty of the elegant Mach 2 aircraft — and close-up the build quality appeared as perfection.

This wasn't quite the same with the amazing SR-71 spy plane that I saw as a guest of Ed de Bertha and Maury Rosenberg in its hangar at RAF Mildenhall. The all-titanium SR-71 seemed very rough in comparison and it dripped JP7 fuel as it sat there. The Lockheed 'skunk works' team who looked after it explained that this was quite normal since the aircraft got so hot in flight that the panels expanded and sealed off the leaks. But to spend a day with the pilots and team at Mildenhall was an amazing privilege. The entire United States Air Force personnel appeared incredibly smart with the exception of the 'skunk works' team, who were making a deliberately casual statement — several had severely non-military pigtails!

All this reminded me of the day with *Thrust2* at Black Rock when we were overflown by an SR-71 and we all waved and cheered for the cameras. I left Mildenhall with mixed feelings, bitterly regretting my career choice.

So back to November 22nd, 1987. I made it on time to Concorde check-in at Heathrow Terminal Four and found myself amongst many famous faces. I had resolved to keep a log of all the flights and the first flight log shows the speed at which everything happened. This was the pinnacle of efficient, luxurious and speedy air travel — I doubt we will ever experience anything like this again in my lifetime.

The runway acceleration to 200mph was quite something, very similar to *Thrust 2* with the incredible, relentless push from the afterburning Olympus engines. But *Thrust 2* could only have two people aboard. With Concorde it was 100 passengers and twice a day out of Heathrow.

Here is that first flight log (UK times throughout):

10.24	Boarding complete
10.30	Start engines
10.42	Line up runway 28 Left
10.43	Rotate wheels off, 217 knots, 250mph
10.50	Mach 0.76, 13,500ft
10.56	Mach 0.95, 28,000ft
11.01	Mach 1.0, 28,000ft
11.28	Mach 2.0, 49,500ft
14.00	US coastline in sight
14.06	Touchdown Kennedy
Flight time	3 hours 21 minutes
Distance	3,129 nautical miles
G-BOAA	

Captain Brian Walpole

Halfway through the flight, a red-faced, bespectacled character in a tweed jacket bent over my seat.

"Your name Noble? Hello, I am John King, chairman of this mob — good luck with the attempt."

On arrival, as instructed, I was first out of the door and ran like hell down the tunnel to the special immigration and customs post where, with a great cheer and flourish, the immigration team stamped my passport, and then I ran down the next-door tunnel to G-BOAG, BA-002. This time things were different — I was greeted by the Concorde purser.

"You don't want to sit in the cabin — that's boring. Captain John Cook wants you to join him in the cockpit."

So far we were on time but there were delays at Kennedy and we didn't start engines until 14.27. With the visor down and the ramp fuel weight of 85,000kg we taxied out, which appeared a very difficult procedure since the cockpit is a long way ahead of the nose wheel and the ride in the cockpit is very rough.

There was more congestion and it wasn't until 14.59 when we rotated on Runway 31L and immediately initiated the famous 25-degree left bank at 50ft and in full afterburner — this was real fighter performance.

On this flight we reached 55,000ft and from the cockpit you could see 350 miles on either side. The usual cumulus clouds seemed a very long way below and the curvature of the earth very apparent. Nightfall came up very rapidly because we were retreating from the sunshine at twice the speed the Earth rotates. Outside the temperature fell to −65 degrees C but the temperature on Concorde's nose was the maximum allowable +127 degrees C due to the very high friction from the airflow.

I was back in the cockpit for the night approach into

Heathrow. We had to fly a hold at Ockham, Surrey due to air-traffic delays and then we were on night finals into Heathrow. At this point there was a message for me in the cockpit: John King's luggage had been left behind and could I make sure it was loaded for the next flight!

The night approach was the most amazing experience and for me, a low-hours private pilot, a very uncomfortable one. The visor was down and the nose drooped, so the view from the cockpit was perfection. As the Concorde slowed, we adopted a very nose-high attitude — and in a light aircraft the combination of slow speed and high nose spells big danger. The Heathrow runway appeared too short and I wondered how on earth we were going to land in time as we were doing 190mph and seemed to be far too high — but at this point the cockpit was 37ft higher than the main wheels. We touched down really smoothly, a real greaser, but then we had to get the nose wheel onto the ground and, with the reverse-thrust braking, the nose and we in the cockpit seemed to be in freefall. The fall seemed to be much too far and I wondered for an instant if we actually had the nose wheel down below us. But we did, and we taxied slowly to the stand. I marvelled at how the captain drove it with the nose wheel and the rest of the aircraft so far behind us. We were down at 18.32. Time to find BA-003.

Flight time for G-BOAG was 3 hours 33 minutes, distance was 3,151 nautical miles and average speed was 887mph.

The return flight to Kennedy in G-BOAE rotated at 19.19 local time and we were back at Kennedy at 22.30. Captain Keith Barton did a superb job and completed the flight in 3 hours 25 minutes, averaging 925mph.

The three trips including transit times totalled 11 hours 22 minutes and 12 hundredths of a second. The average speed including the stops was 864mph.

The next stop was Mortimer's in New York for the BA celebration party, where I was met by John King.

"Nice of you to go back and collect my luggage!"

On Tuesday morning I was back in the ARV office at Blackbushe.

"Did you have a fulfilling weekend?" asked Bruce Giddings.

"Yes, I crossed the Atlantic four times!"

And there was absolutely no jet lag — it was as if I had just driven to the office.

CHAPTER 5

ATLANTIC SPRINTER

"I really like this marine project of yours, Richard. It uses Shell jet fuel and our oil tanker captains would love it. Do we know whether the engine is any good?"

Marketing Director, Shell UK

ARV Aviation was coming to an end. There was to be no more funding from City bankers and it seemed a very wasteful situation to have a certificated aircraft, a production facility and a vast number of sales enquiries — and just give up on the programme because it was going through engineering difficulties that could easily be fixed. Certainly the ARV Isle of Wight team had a great deal more faith and resilience than the City people, but without funding the programme could only last so long. The project went into administration and was bought by ARV's financial director.

About this time, Adrian Hamilton, an old friend, had an incredible idea and called a small team together for a lunch. The project was to be called *Atlantic Sprinter*.

Adrian explained that the Hales Trophy is the most famous marine trophy for the fastest crossing of the Atlantic starting at the Ambrose Light, New York and timed to the Scilly Isles. Before airliners crossed the Atlantic, there was a massive volume of passenger ship traffic and great competition to establish the best crossing time. The fastest ship had two great advantages: it could attract premium ticket prices; and with careful management it could complete more transatlantic trips in a year. The record breakers were known as Blue Riband holders, a title initiated in the 1890s.

The Hales Trophy, donated by Harold Hales of Coventry, became the Blue Riband trophy for passenger vessels. It was fought for continuously from 1936 and was held by famous liners such as SS *Normandie* and RMS *Queen Mary*. The fastest liner of all was the SS *United States*, which achieved a record speed of 34.51 knots in 1952. The current Hales Trophy holder is *Cat-Link V* at 41.3 knots, established in 1998.

The Hales Trophy was all but forgotten when Ted Toleman and Richard Branson decided to challenge in a high-performance Cougar catamaran as an unusual way of promoting the Virgin Atlantic airline. There was no way in which they could carry the entire fuel load for the job so they elected to refuel from support vessels stationed along the route. The Cougar attempt failed when the boat, *Challenger*, broke up. But Richard commissioned another refuelled racer, *Challenger II*, and completed the job with a record of 36 knots, generating massive publicity and interest. However, the Hales people refused Richard the Hales Trophy on the grounds that the boat was not a commercial vessel and that it had been refuelled on the way. Richard responded by creating his own trophy.

But there were developing rumours that His Royal Highness the Aga Khan was commissioning a massive racer to attempt the record without refuelling. This would give the Hales Committee something of a left-field challenge — they would have to decide whether to award their trophy for the fastest unrefuelled crossing whether commercial or not. Given the scale of the Aga Khan's programme, it was questionable whether the Hales Trophy really mattered — the fastest would be the fastest and the Hales Trophy might just become a historical footnote.

Our *Atlantic Sprinter* team decided to advance the programme with careful steps. It was a truly beautiful design and a large boardroom model was produced. It attracted huge interest and Adrian's chosen designer believed it could do the job based on his previous experience of high-speed race boat and yacht design. The risk was substantial: if it failed, the vessel would be stranded in the Atlantic and attract all kinds of salvage offers with massive loss of sponsor prestige. The team also faced a serious problem: how could they prove to would-be sponsors that the vessel could do the job? The answer was far from straight-forward and hull-form design (design of the wet parts of a boat hull) in those days was a black art. As the *Sprinter* team and the designer were unable to prove the mathematics, the entire programme became a massive gamble based on trust. By contrast, Richard Branson's programme had been a much better, low-risk promotional bet.

The *Sprinter* team were lost. It was truly a great and inspiring idea but not having the ability to prove the performance was stranding the project.

I raised the subject with my old friend John Scott, a highly experienced Rolls-Royce propulsion engineer who had been in charge of the Rolls-Royce/British Aerospace HOTOL (HOrizontal Take-Off & Landing) next-generation orbital transport. He was also one of the founders of the SABRE (Synergetic Air Breathing Rocket Engine) programme at Alan Bond's Reaction Engines. I broached the subject with Scottie.

"What do we do? It's a brilliant idea but we can't

progress unless we can prove range and speed?"

Of course, the answer was simple, coming from a truly great engineer.

"In the aerospace industry we always had that problem until Louis Breguet came up with the famous range equation, which enabled us to predict the absolute range of an aircraft."

John joined us at the next meeting and I brought along my heavy grey-coloured IBM XT computer. We loaded it with Monsieur Breguet's equation and then in front of the team inputted the boat's design variables. The beautiful boat would not make it across the Atlantic — the designer was appalled.

We were saved from public humiliation since we had not published the project and the team now had to find a high-technology way forward — or leave the stage to the Aga Khan. Meanwhile, the Italians were coming up with their unrefuelled project, the *Azimut Atlantic Challenger*, and in America Tom Gentry was building *Gentry Eagle* with two diesel engines and a gas turbine. The challenge was hotting up and looked like becoming a race.

John Scott took control.

"To do this, we need a special low-drag hull form and a very efficient powerplant. The boat hull needs to be strong enough to deal with the Atlantic weather and yet lightweight — so we need to innovate big-time on shape, structure and power plant."

Curiously this all came together reasonably quickly, just as details of the Aga Khan's massive 67-metre *Destriero* became public. He was using conventional boat technology with 60,000 horsepower and a massive 400-tonne displacement. He was planning an average speed of 50 knots.

We wanted 60 knots average. If *Destriero* represented the peak of conventional performance, then we would have to innovate on a truly massive scale that could change an entire industry!

We quickly learned that the marine industry is super-conventional and risk-adverse with very good reason. Hull design is something of a black art, engines have to perform in aggressive seas, and boat structural failure can lead to loss of life in appalling conditions.

But as Charles Lindbergh said about flying the Atlantic, you have to keep trying again and again until the challenge is conquered.

The first sign of progress was a meeting with Erbil Serter, a very experienced Turkish designer who had been focusing on a different sort of hull form — a high-speed, semi-displacement shape that does not plane and relies on a deep bow shape to keep the bow in the water and ensure a constant waterline length, thus minimising wave drag.

The Serter design also includes a deep-vee hull cross-section, so designed that as the boat progresses the water rides up each side of the vee until it meets the longitudinal chines where it curves over to create a couple of longitudinal vortices, one on each side of the boat. The longitudinal vortex on each side stabilises the long, thin, low-drag hull in roll by means of, as one genius described it, "a couple of rolled-up carpets". This enables the boat to be longer and thinner than otherwise might be possible. The keel is cranked so that the aft section of the hull runs at a greater incidence when compared with the front half; this does the job of keeping the stern half of the boat from sinking down at speed and increasing hydro drag.

At first we were stunned by the complexity but then, with Serter's help, we ran his hull form, the Serter 6X-B, for two full days at various speeds, sea states and displacements at the huge HSVA test tank in Hamburg. We were deeply impressed. The tests resulted in reams of data and reports. Later, with the help of RAE Bedford, we were able to take the vertical accelerations from the HSVA tank runs and experience them for real in the cockpit simulator — it was a comfortable ride and very workable. So we had a start for the boat hull that would handle the speed and the variable displacement as the fuel load was burned off operating in the Sea State 4 wave conditions we had specified.

The next stage was the engine. John Scott believed we should be headed for a modern lightweight gas-turbine engine of some 30,000 horsepower — about half that of the *Destriero*. He chose the Rolls-Royce RB211-22B that powered the Lockheed Tristar airliner. John's plan was to remove the fan from the front of the engine and take the turbine drive forward to a large GEC bespoke gearbox that in turn would drive four surface-piercing water propellers. The propellers were specifically designed for the project by the famous marine propeller designer Phil Rolla, whose propeller designs were unbeatable — just like his Italian family cooking! In addition, a huge breakthrough was achieved by Pat Dallard of Ove Arup who devised a way of building the hull in extruded aluminium planks, which, when welded side by side, would result in a very smooth monocoque construction in which the hull loading would be taken by the hull sides, minimising both weight and internal structure. Norsk Hydro were interested and started extruding the aluminium test planks for the carvel construction method. The boat would be built like an aeroplane — very light and very strong. This combination, John believed, would give us the fuel efficiency, the low hydro drag and the lightness and strength necessary for the job.

Rolls-Royce, by coincidence, were restoring an early RB211 jumbo jet engine in Derby for a museum and they were prepared to make it available for the project. The engine actually had my name on it. The deal just needed high-level board approval. At first they said it was going to be all right. I sat in the office for two solid weeks waiting for the final telephone call Rolls-Royce had promised — and it came eventually. It was negative: they didn't want to risk the company's reputation for aviation safety by using the RB211 engine in an experimental marine application.

So with no engine, the highly promising project was over. I had no idea how to acquire such a huge engine and the little team certainly hadn't the funds to buy one. By coincidence I was due to go on a family holiday in Cornwall and we set off. The break didn't last long: a specialist engine dealer called.

"Richard, are you after an RB211?"

"That's right — and we have failed with Rolls-Royce."

"Well, I know where there are four..."

"OK, very funny... hanging on the wings of a jumbo jet at Heathrow!"

"No, I'm being serious, Richard. This is your chance — they're in a scrapyard at Shifnal."

I turned to Sally.

"I have to go to Shifnal. It will just take one day..."

I started early for Shifnal, in Shropshire, and found the scrapyard, which was dominated by four huge jumbo engines. Three were wrecks but the fourth looked good and it appeared to have new fan blades.

I tried to negotiate but I was outclassed: the fourth engine had already been sold.

So I went back to Cornwall.

I was working on something else when I got a strange call.

"Hello, I'm Henry. I'm the one who bought the jumbo engine in Shifnal. Look, I have decided to make some changes in my business, and if you want the engine, I'll sell it to you."

One evening that week we borrowed the engine support team from British Airways Heathrow and 'borescoped' the engine, looking into its internals with special video probes and tools.

"It looks amazingly good!" they said.

The next week I had the key meeting with the Marketing Director at Shell.

"I really like this marine project of yours, Richard. It uses Shell jet fuel and our oil tanker captains would love it. Do we know whether the engine is any good?"

"There's only one way to prove it to you — we'll get it run up for you!"

I went back to the head of propulsion at British Airways.

"Can we borrow a test cell one evening to run up our RB211?"

He was amazingly tactful.

"We can't do that, Richard. If your engine were to blow, it would take out our test cell and that would screw up our entire engine programme. I really want to help, but I also don't want your engine here in case some of your engine parts find themselves onto our engines."

Of course, he meant the reverse!

There was only one more chance — I had met the head of propulsion at Cranfield University some months before and he was enjoying himself testing small gas turbines for the students. I explained that this was his once-in-a-lifetime chance to run up a serious jumbo engine.

"Right, let's get it done…"

The Cranfield engineers quickly whipped up a vast engine stand using steel I-beams. We sent up the engine on a low loader and bolted the stand to a concrete road and connected the huge engine. The RAE Bedford team provided two air-start units and a bifurcated air-start pipe to link the two units with some of the most beautiful welding I have ever seen.

January 21st, 1989 was a very cold Sunday morning when the British Airways engine team joined us on the Cranfield airfield. The huge 9ft-diameter RB211 standing out at the end of the airfield was connected up, checked out and ready to run.

The first start nearly got there and there were clouds of blue smoke.

"Good sign," said the engine team. "That's the oil — its systems have been inhibited."

The second start was brilliant. The huge engine roared into life and settled down to a beautifully smooth idle. The British Airways team had broad smiles on their faces. They opened up the throttle but didn't get very far because the concrete road started to move, so we never got beyond flight idle. We clearly had a very good engine.

Two days later I was back with the British Airways head of propulsion. I put a video player on his desk and his eyes nearly popped out of his head. The video showed the runs and finished showing the engine winding down and the team of 30 all cheering at the huge achievement.

It took the head of propulsion just a second or two to catch on…

"Those are all my people!"

"Yes, we borrowed them on Sunday. They weren't doing anything. I hope you don't mind…"

"How can I help you?"

"Well, we need the engine logs — we own the engine so we should be supplied with the records."

As happens in the extraordinary world of commercial aviation, British Airways and Rolls-Royce had a major conference… in Hong Kong. Somehow the logs were found. Our engine, it seemed, was the RB211-22B certified testbed engine, recently overhauled and with very few running hours. No one seemed to know how this valuable engine had been cast out by Rolls-Royce along with the engine wrecks.

But the Rolls-Royce main board had got wind of the project and immediately issued a company-wide edict that no Rolls-Royce staff were to be involved. At least someone was taking the *Sprinter* team seriously.

With the main components of the *Sprinter* now

found, if not paid for, we could progress to a public launch. This was done at London's Mermaid Theatre, where we even had the huge RB211 beautifully polished up and on the stage. There was massive interest in this extraordinary and innovative programme.

We had an interesting foretaste of public interest at the *Daily Express* Boat Show in London, where we displayed the engine and showed videos of the development of the Serter hull in the HSVA tank. The boat-buying public were fascinated but showed little interest or understanding in the extreme technology.

Now we had to build it. We talked with various British yards who explained that they didn't take risks and it was for the government to fund it. The Department of Trade & Industry were the people supposed to take the risk, but they were even more risk-adverse than the yards.

However, Vosper in Southampton were fascinated by the programme, which, if it went their way, would give them a world lead in the next generation of high-speed blue-water patrol boats. With a very thin order book, Vosper had laid off most of their workforce but had a substantial bank balance. Signing up with *Sprinter* would give them priceless access to the new technology, employ their workforce and open up a new market.

But the directors were not biting. Many years later the managing director admitted that they had made a serious mistake.

We at last found real interest in Newcastle, past home of British shipbuilding. *Sprinter* would be built on the Tyne and there were potential sponsors. The Shell lead had gone quiet but the local brewery, Scottish & Newcastle, was prepared to use the boat to promote its Newcastle Brown Ale worldwide. A location for the build yard was found at the Newcastle Garden Festival site and the Rubb assembly hall was erected on its special concrete base. But that's as far as the project got because Britain suddenly slipped into deep recession and there was a complete collapse of the sponsorship market. Both the *Daily Express* and the brewery helped us clear up the financial mess.

But now a German yard, Abeking & Rasmussen, started to show interest. This was credible interest because the yard had already built Serter military designs with some success. So the entire *Sprinter* team turned up in Bremen to meet the Abeking & Rasmussen people and the outcome of two days of talks was positive. They agreed to build the boat but they wanted an engine guarantee from Rolls-Royce. Given the Rolls-Royce board's edict to employees, that was something we could never deliver and so the project ended.

Many years later I was at a wedding in Scotland and met the Scottish & Newcastle chairman, now retired.

"Richard, now that I see your team has broken the Sound Barrier, I completely understand what *Atlantic Sprinter* could have done for the north-east. We should have backed you properly — please accept my apologies."

In 1992 *Destriero* crossed the Atlantic on the eastbound track of 3,106 nautical miles in 58 hours, 34 minutes and 5 seconds — averaging 53.09 knots. But even the Aga Khan didn't get the Hales Trophy as it was still reserved for commercial vessels. Even so, it was a very great achievement.

Looking back on all this, *Destriero* might have done even better if it had been chased by the *Atlantic Sprinter*. This would have been the greatest boat race of all time with massive global coverage for the sponsors. It so very nearly happened.

CHAPTER 6
PROGRAMME FUNDING

"OK, we'll get you £1.5 million in three months if you'll give us the deal."

Richard Noble, 'The Big Race'

In 1993, trading prospects were bleak. Britain was back in a recession and everything seemed to be going backward. With no work available, I painted our Hampton home and nearly lost my footing on the scaffolding. But business has the habit of emerging and this time from the most unlikely source — the Rolls-Royce Enthusiasts' Club in Paulerspury, Northamptonshire. It was about the 1914 Alpenfahrt.

The Rolls-Royce Enthusiasts' Club is exactly what it says on the box. It is dedicated to the owners of these beautiful vintage heirlooms and cares for over 100,000 production records of these hand-built cars. Back in 1914, Rolls-Royce achieved lasting fame in Europe by winning the Alpenfahrt, a mighty 2,930-kilometre

Alpine mountain race through Austria, Switzerland, Italy and Croatia. The man of the match was James Radley, Rolls-Royce test driver and curiously also holder of the World Air Speed Record. The challenge was so important to Rolls-Royce at that time that they created a special car, the Alpine Eagle, a really beautiful and much sought-after lightweight racer.

Part of the Rolls-Royce Enthusiasts' Club's DNA is absolute, obsessional detail and the plan was to rerun the 1914 Alpenfahrt on its 80th anniversary and remind the world of Rolls-Royce's success in an extraordinarily tough race where the Alpine Eagles triumphed in grand style, coming in first, second and third against the best in the world.

The club had researched the subject in great depth and the members were becoming excited. There were just two problems — no television coverage and no sponsorship. It took a huge effort to get the BBC interested, but when they realised the scale on which this was being executed, with perfect Rolls-Royces from all over the world being flown into Austria for the start, they became excited. But there was one more difficulty: the event had to be sponsored and the BBC couldn't cope with evil commerce blighting their programmes.

Somehow we got the proposal through and Motorola

sponsored — and they got a bargain. The most beautiful Rolls-Royces were shipped in from all over and the club went to extreme lengths of re-enactment, with an exact restoration of the 1914-winning Alpine Eagle and with its owner adopting the clothing and persona of Mr Radley. Funds raised went to the Red Cross to fund a much-needed hospital in Croatia and Rolls-Royce enthusiasts now have a documentary programme they can replay for ever.

But the television world was suffering from the recession and producers were finding it difficult to fund new programmes. Ray Stewart, a *Daily Express* director, had an idea: why not pioneer commercial funding of television programmes? I was proud to join the Programme Funding team.

I found the television world a really difficult culture to master. There were huge sums of money involved and the massive bureaucracy was both byzantine and difficult to understand. Above all we were not television people and it showed because we couldn't talk the language and had no production pedigree. I found it hard to get excited about the potential of cartoon characters. But being outsiders with different experience should have helped at a time when the television world was going through financial convulsions.

Ray had managed to get some start-up seed investment so Programme Funding could exist for the short term, and the ideas were good and often very clever, but we were suffering the usual pain of a new start-up. How do we get that first big deal?

The story was an extraordinary one. Richard Creasey, a television producer, had created a major international incident with *Death of a Princess*, a programme which, to put it mildly, exposed major Middle East cultural differences resulting in extreme political repercussions. He was keen to replicate the excitement of his upbringing, when his famous father, the novelist John Creasey, would load the family and books in his car and they would travel all over the world selling his novels, leaving a trail of enthusiastic readers.

Richard had even bigger ideas. He realised that there would be a brief instant in the construction of the Channel Tunnel when, just before the rails went down, it would be possible to drive a car through it. There also existed a strange spider-like Russian amphibious vessel called the Arktos that could swim in Arctic waters and climb out onto the floating ice. Therefore, Richard triumphantly reasoned, for a very short, never-to-be-repeated window, it would be possible to drive from London to New York, via the Channel Tunnel,

Moscow and the pack ice of the Bering Strait. It was to be called 'The Big Race'.

A complex financial deal had been done between regional television franchise broadcasters Central Television (Midlands) and Meridian Television (South and South-East) to support the programme series and at least fund the research — and that's where it ran into trouble. The route involved researching the drive through Siberia in winter before the ice melted and crossing the Bering Strait in the Arktos swimmer to reach Alaska for a highway drive to New York. The research was extremely expensive, involving many hours of Siberian helicopter travel. With his indefatigable motivation, Richard had completed the research but it had yet to be paid for — and for some reason it was on Meridian's balance sheet.

So here we had a number of people and organisations in potential trouble — Richard because his reputation was on the line, Meridian because it was stuck with the debt, and Programme Funding because it had failed to achieve its first deal. There were at least seven one-hour national peak-time programmes on offer for the series.

Meridian had decided that programme sponsorship was the solution — but the television people they had appointed hadn't been able to land the deal. Programme

Funding was now in desperate straits with no successes and Meridian was coming up to year end with this huge debt on its balance sheet.

We eventually fought our way through to a meeting with the Meridian CEO, who had reached a point of some desperation where he would listen to anyone — even us.

Meridian CEO: "We have this huge debt on our balance sheet."

Programme Funding: "This is what we do — how much do you really need?"

Meridian: "We need at least £800,000 to clear the debt."

Programme Funding: "OK, we'll get you £1.5 million in three months if you'll give us the rights to raise the funds."

The CEO's eyes nearly popped out of his head and with no other options he signed.

Much of the credit for all this went to Ray Stewart and his promotional film, which featured music from Queen and extraordinary scenes of extreme human achievement including famous footage of a Land Rover winching itself up the outside of a massive concrete dam.

Ford were about to launch their Mondeo 'world car' and this could be their world promotion. We presented to the board and I was amazed by the sheer selling power of Ray's film. Later I had a call from the Ford director.

"Jac's seen it and has agreed it is to go ahead. Congratulations on a really good sales pitch — we enjoyed it." 'Jac' was Jac Nasser, Chairman of Ford Europe.

Richard Creasey got his programme, Ford got their enormous media exposure and Meridian got the programming as well as having the debt cleared. The programme, called *The Big Race: Overland to America* and broadcast in seven key Thursday evening slots, achieved huge viewing figures.

There was amazing footage of the Ford Mondeos fighting their way through the Siberian winter ice and impossibly deep snow. The Arktos disappointed, which was bad luck, but the team and their Mondeos made it through to the United Nations headquarters in New York on April 5th, 1994, just over three months after their departure from London.

I had to cash in my chips and leave at this point as I couldn't get excited by Programme Funding's next cartoon opportunities. Besides, the speed of sound was looming very large. And then there was this urgent telephone call to take...

CHAPTER 7
SUPERSONIC

"You are setting us up, Richard!"

Jonathan Fry, CEO, Castrol

My old friend Art Arfons of Akron, Ohio had a radical idea. The multiple Land Speed Record holder, universally known as the 'Junkyard Genius of the Jet Set', had built and run 26 racers, dragsters and Land Speed Record challengers powered by huge aero engines. All his cars were known as *Green Monster* after his first, built in 1952, had been finished in left-over tractor paint of that colour. In November 1966 he had survived the world's fastest car accident at over 600mph.

Arfons had now decided to go small, so *Green Monster* number 27 was a minimalist Land Speed Record car that was more like a 650mph cruise missile with Art sitting right up front. He was convinced of the concept and even built himself a personal centrifuge to check his physical capability. Art was always a great performer and this had to be experienced, so I went to Bonneville once again.

But it didn't work out for Art. The ride in the lightweight car with solid wheels on the hard salt was so rough that he suffered from eyeball inertia and couldn't focus. He had to give up. His great 1965 rival, Craig Breedlove, had turned up to share the experience. Breedlove and I were standing around kicking the salt and talking records and engineering when Craig suddenly became serious.

"Richard, I want you to know that I am building the next *Spirit of America*. I have bought the J79 jet engines and I am committed."

"How fast, Craig?"

"Well, put it this way — I was first over 400, first over 500, first over 600 — so now it's 700mph and supersonic!"

So the *Thrust2* record was up for grabs. Breedlove, the great American hero, would have most of his country behind him and, of course, his long-term backers, Shell Oil.

Once back in the UK, I was surprised by the number of similar calls I received from friends in the industry.

"Richard, you ought to know what's going on. We can't tell you because we have signed an NDA [Non-Disclosure Agreement] — but we suggest you had better find out!"

A few days later there was a different type of call, from the McLaren Formula 1 team's PR department.

"We have some sponsors over in 10 days' time and we need to entertain them. We would like to show them your *Thrust2* video — would you send us a VHS copy?"

I promised to send them a copy and... sort of, well, forgot about it...

The following week there was another McLaren call.

"The VHS hasn't arrived!"

"Oh dear, how did that happen? You can't trust the post these days. Let me send you another."

And I sort of forgot about that one too.

The next week the McLaren people were apoplectic. For some extraordinary reason the second VHS had not arrived either. So this time I sent them one and now we knew — there was to be a McLaren Land Speed Record car.

This was going to be a mighty battle and of course we had to engage and challenge — but how?

The answer came from an unexpected quarter. In May 1993 I was called by Castrol and asked to give a presentation on the Castrol brand at their global conference in Palm Springs, California. Their first-choice speaker had dropped out and I was the fallback. We agreed that the presentation was to include Castrol's Land Speed Record heritage.

I was allowed to search the famous Castrol archive. Here I found an amazing exchange between Sir Malcolm Campbell, record breaker of the 1920s and '30s and also a great self-publicist, and Charles Cheers Wakefield, founder of Castrol.

Campbell: 'Dear Charles, I have served your company well and achieved a great many World Records for Castrol — will you make me a director?'

Wakefield: 'Sorry Malcolm, we only recruit internally.'

The entire Castrol board and all of its global senior executives were present at Palm Springs for an occasion held only every five years. I gave them a presentation highlighting Castrol's achievements of the past and suggesting that each generation had to contribute to and invigorate the famous brand. It seemed to go down well and hit the spot with the audience. I walked back and joined the board's table, where Jonathan Fry, Castrol's CEO, was sitting.

"You are setting us up, Richard!" said Jonathan.

deal water at Loch Ness in 1952: John Cobb and *Crusader* preparing for
a high-speed run. *Author's collection*

Thrust1 lies upside-down on the runway at RAF Fairford in 1977 following
a triple roll. The car was sold to a scrap dealer the same day. *Author's collection*

Thrust2 chief designer John Ackroyd with his preferred means of transport, photographed on the Isle of Wight in 1980. He travelled rather more quickly when he rode with me at 400mph on Bonneville Salt Flats. *Author's collection*

The wonderful *Thrust2* team at Black Rock Desert, Nevada, in 1983. Sadly many of these brilliant people are no longer with us. *Author's collection*

Thrust2 sets off in full afterburner mode on the second pass of the Land Speed Record run at Black Rock Desert. On this run the car peaked at 650.88mph — the fastest ever achieved on land at that time. *Alamy*

Thrust2 at rest on Black Rock Desert's cracked surface having just captured the world record for the mile at 633.47mph. *Author's collection*

It's all over! For Britain and for the hell of it! I am interviewed by Rob Widdows, with Sally and daughter Genevieve on the right. *Author's collection*

Thrust2 is now displayed at the Coventry Transport Museum. *Stefan Marjoram*

Initiated without money or an engine, the ARV Super2 took just 13 months from start-up to first flight. Test pilot Don Ellis flies number 12, which later belonged to me. *Author's collection*

We passed the exam! The Chairman of the Civil Aviation Authority, Sir John Dent, hands me the official CAA Type Certificate, which clears the design for production — one of the most difficult team challenges imaginable. As soon as British Airways learned that the CAA Chairman was on site, they rolled up a Concorde. Flying the three ARVs out of Heathrow was a scary experience. *Author's collection*

Engine coolant pump failure in my beloved ARV Super2, G-BMWE, meant a forced landing — thankfully in a handy field. The superplastic aluminium forward structure saved my life. *Author's collection*

133

As drawn in 1987, this was the final shape of *Atlantic Sprinter*, using the Serter 6XB semi-displacement hull and a Rolls-Royce RB211-22 powerplant. The target was to cross the Atlantic at an average speed of 60 knots. *Author's collection*

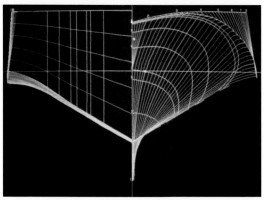

Martin Francis's design work on the Serter 6XB hull enabled a long, thin, deep, vee-shaped semi-displacement profile with a varying-incidence keel line. The chines convert lateral flow into longitudinal vortices to provide lateral stability. *Author's collection*

The Serter 6X-B hull on test at the HSVA test tank in Hamburg, where two full days of assessment revealed great promise. The photo shows the deep-vee semi-displacement hull transom section and the longitudinal vortices for stability in roll. *Author's collection*

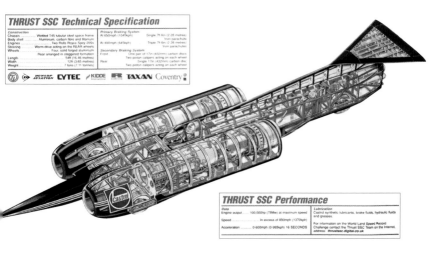

THRUST SSC Technical Specification

Construction
Chassis — Welded T45 tubular steel space frame
Body shell — Aluminium, carbon fibre and titanium
Engines — Two Rolls-Royce Spey 205s
Steering — Worm drive acting on the REAR wheels
Wheels — Four, solid forged aluminium
Rear arranged in staggered formation
Length — 54ft (16.46 metres)
Width — 12ft (3.65 metres)
Weight — 7 tons (7.11 tonnes)

Primary Braking System
At 650mph (1047kph) — Single 7ft 6in (2.28 metres)
twin parachute
At 400mph (643kph) — Triple 7ft 6in (2.28 metres)
twin parachutes

Secondary Braking System
Front — One pair of 17in (432mm) carbon discs
Two piston calipers acting on each wheel
Rear — Single 17in (432mm) carbon disc
Two piston calipers acting on each wheel

THRUST SSC Performance

Data
Engine output — 100,000hp (75Mw) at maximum speed
Speed — In excess of 850mph (1370kph)
Acceleration — 0-600mph (0-965kph) 16 SECONDS

Lubrication
Castrol synthetic lubricants, brake fluids, hydraulic fluids and greases.

For information on the World Land Speed Record Challenge contact the Thrust SSC Team on the Internet, address: thrustssc.digital.co.uk

Castrol issued this *ThrustSSC* poster showing the cutaway work of Lawrie Watts. The structural frame designed by Glynne Bowsher can be clearly seen together with the twin Rolls-Royce Spey 202 Phantom engines and the rear-wheel-steer arrangement. Andy Green's cockpit is in the ideal position, in the safest part of the car and close to the centre of gravity. *Author's collection*

The start of the *ThrustSSC* Computational Fluid Dynamics programme at Swansea University — the first time high-performance car aerodynamics had been evaluated by CFD. *Author's collection*

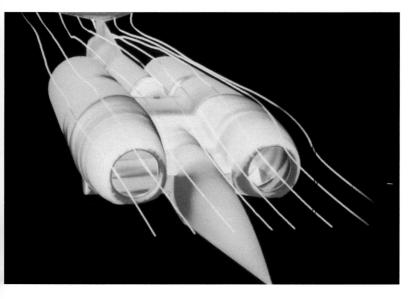

As CFD was new technology, there was uncertainty about the validity of the results, so multiple rocket-test runs were made on the Long Test Track at MoD Pendine in South Wales — an innovative use of this facility for aerodynamic testing. The rocket's acceleration time for 0–820mph was 0.8 second.
MoD Pendine

Ron Ayers plotted the CFD results against the Pendine test data. The straight line shows an amazing correlation — both methods produced almost identical outcomes. This was the point at which *ThrustSSC* could advance with aerodynamic confidence.
Courtesy of Ron Ayers

ThrustSSC in Jordan for the second time, in 1997. King Hussein gave the team use of the Al-Jafr Desert for high-speed development runs so we could try to catch up with Craig Breedlove's *Spirit of America* team, which could only run in the US. Our fastest speed in Jordan was 540mph.
Motorsport Images/Sutton

ThrustSSC on Black Rock Desert in October 1997 after one of the faster runs; the car is surrounded by American followers who camped on the hills. *Author's collection*

Microlight pilot Richard Meredith-Hardy took this amazing photo of *ThrustSSC* at supersonic speed. Following overnight rain, the low sun picks up the surface dust raised by the supersonic shockwave. *Richard Meredith-Hardy*

Begun in 2002, the Farnborough F1 project was an attempt to provide business passengers with a fast, bespoke, low-cost regional travel service, operating Uber-like between the small airfields that are so numerous in America and Europe. *Author's collection*

The Farnborough F1 programme was acquired by Kestrel Aircraft Company in the US and subsequently sold to One Aviation, which shelved the project in 2018. *Author's collection*

Dieselmax, the world's fastest diesel, was created by JCB to showcase the company's new engine. Based on the layout of John Cobb's *Railton Mobil Special*, the car had aerodynamics by Ron Ayers. It was driven by Andy Green to a timed record of 350.092mph on Bonneville Salt Flats. *JCB*

Andy Green: RAF fighter pilot (with 3,000 hours of fast-jet time), Fastest Man on Earth, and key driver and enabler of *ThrustSSC*, *Dieselmax* and *BloodhoundSSC*. Andy's exceptional courage and quiet determination made these projects possible. The *ThrustSSC* and *Dieselmax* records have never been broken. *Stefan Marjoram*

Ron Ayers: without his aerodynamic expertise, *ThrustSSC*, *Dieselmax* and *BloodhoundSSC* would never even have started. Ron's experience, patience and team skills were an essential part of these projects and he generated high levels of confidence amongst team and sponsors. *Author's collection*

The 130,000-horsepower *BloodhoundSSC* under construction at its Bristol base. With 300 sponsors, 37,000 names on the tail fin and engaging with 120,000 youngsters per annum, the project fell at the last fence due to a delayed government financial commitment. *Stefan Marjoram*

The *Bloodhound* Engineering team managed by Chris Fairhead and including Chief Engineer Mark Chapman. *Stefan Marjoram*

BloodhoundSSC wheels at Bristol. The low-speed wheel has a Dunlop Lightning tyre for 200mph demonstration runs on British runways. The unique high-speed wheel is the work of 20 companies, including Lockheed Martin, with machining done by Castle Precision Engineering in Glasgow. *Stefan Marjoram*

The *Bloodhound* Education programme was highly successful and it was a huge privilege for me to be part of it. *Stefan Marjoram*

Andy Green, Ron Ayers and me with the superbly supportive executive committee of the South African Northern Cape government. Under their leadership, 1,000 'man years' of work went into the preparation of the special Hakskeenpan desert track. *Stefan Marjoram*

BloodhoundSSC on its way to Newquay in 2017 for its first public demonstration runs, attended by 10,000 visitors. Arthur Spriggs & Sons most generously provided transportation for the project and its education team. *Stefan Marjoram*

Andy Green and *BloodhoundSSC* blast away for another 200mph run at Newquay. This exercise, a huge success, was followed every hour by the BBC, and live streaming from Cisco took all the action to a global audience. *Stefan Marjoram*

We were not the only ones building a *BloodhoundSSC* car (below left) and sharing the dream! Ten years of *BloodhoundSSC* promotion generated huge media coverage (below right), with a return to the sponsors valued at £1.5 billion. *Stefan Marjoram*

In October 2018 we had to put *BloodhoundSSC* into Administration. It was bought by Ian Warhurst, who intends to see the project through to completion — he has a great team, a great car and a great opportunity to make a mighty big statement for Britain. *Author's collection*

Reid Railton's original 1954 tank-test model of *Crusader 2* undergoes scanning by aerospace specialist company Addqual in Derby. From Addqual's work, the design has been converted to drawings for construction of jet test models by Len Newton. *Author's collection*

"Of course, Jonathan!"

"Come and see us when you get back!" said Brian Ridgewell, one of the directors.

It was dark in the London basement office of Programme Funding when the phone rang. Brian Ridgewell was back in the UK.

"I have £40,000 unspent on the marketing budget. Would that be helpful in getting you started?"

Curiously, the M25 motorway around London made an immeasurable contribution to the *ThrustSSC* project. The road's designers hadn't allowed for local people using it for quick, local, short-cut travel and there were tremendous accidents and congestion. Ken Norris was having an open day at his flying club in Bournemouth and I was late for it because of a log-jam on the M25 — and because I was late I met Ron Ayers there.

Ken introduced me to Ron, who opened with a question I couldn't answer.

"Why do all these Land Speed Record cars under-perform?"

Ron had been head of aerodynamics at the huge Bristol Aeroplane plant at Filton and was now a public guide at Brooklands, where he had access to the wind tunnel records from the 1930s. It seemed that even R.J.

Mitchell, designer of the Spitfire, had been active on Land Speed Record car designs.

In the immediate post-war period, Britain led the world in aircraft design and manufacture. With the onset of the Cold War, the government realised the importance of achieving supersonic aviation and commissioned the Miles aircraft company in Reading to produce the first ever supersonic design. The Miles 52 was to be powered by a Whittle jet engine and the programme was some 80 per cent through its funding when the government got cold feet, overruled the very competent design team and cancelled the programme before the aircraft flew.

This left the way clear for the United States. Following the first supersonic achievements of test pilot George Welch in the North American XP-86, the United States Air Force formally claimed the first supersonic flight with Chuck Yeager in the Bell X-1. When news of this secret project eventually leaked out, it seemed that the British appeared to have wimped out and handed the intellectual lead to our American friends. It was to cost the British a 10-year lead in the aviation industry.

So apart from the need to right the wrongs of 1947, there was now a tremendous battle in prospect for the first supersonic Land Speed Record with credible challenges from Breedlove and McLaren — and we hadn't even started.

Ron Ayers 'sort of just started' on the supersonic car project: he wanted to see whether the outline design was remotely viable. He brought his large slide rule out of retirement, acquired a desktop computer and was operational within days. He made the quick decision to pioneer the use of Computational Fluid Dynamics and to work with the new CFD team at Swansea University under the management of Professor Oubay Hassan. There were obvious problems: the university's central computer had minimal available capacity and time, but Cray Research came to our aid with the loan of a Cray 92, which sped up the processing. At about this time the project was also helped along by the Russians because the SALT Treaty (Strategic Arms Limitation Talks) had been signed and the Royal Air Force had to dismantle its Phantom fighter fleet — there were afterburning Spey engines available. Rick Jones generously put up the money and so we had two good Spey engines — and the project could start.

The new car was to be called *ThrustSSC* — we wanted to make it plain that we intended to achieve supersonic performance.

But with innovation there are always massive and unpredictable side issues that leave you wondering how you are ever going to get out of the bear pit.

One of the first came from Glynne Bowsher, a highly competent engineer who had designed the all-important wheel brakes for *Thrust2* and was busy designing structure, wheels and running gear for *ThrustSSC*. We all met up at the RAF Museum at Cosford to examine the Bristol 188 stainless-steel supersonic research aircraft of the 1960s — a very similar design to *ThrustSSC*. Glynne had come to a conclusion and put it in his quiet but decisive manner.

"We can't steer the front wheels because there's no space for the steering-gear structure and I'm also concerned that gyroscopic precession from the wheels might roll the car at high speed. [If displaced, gyros have an inexplicable habit of generating massive forces in a direction 90 degrees to the direction of displacement]. So we will have to rear-wheel steer the car..."

This was a bombshell. At the start of any project you are always looking out for the show-stoppers that would make the project unachievable or downright dangerous. Rear-wheel steering is thought to be dangerous and in practice is restricted to slow-speed vehicles such as dumper trucks and mobile cranes. To complete the project, we would have to create a rear-steer supersonic vehicle and overcome the new driving skill requirement, and the engineering and publicity bias, together with sponsor concerns. This was all going uphill and becoming very, very difficult.

Ron also had a problem. The CFD work from Swansea was showing that the new car had good performance and stability but he had real concern about the credibility of the new technology. He had approached the project from a position of interested and unbiased judgement and he was aware that we were creating a vehicle that could, in the wrong hands, be a killer. He wanted a second opinion on the aero work, not from another specialist but from a completely different perspective.

This was becoming very difficult — and seriously sticky when short of money and surrounded by a swamp of uncertainty. We knew that our well-funded competition could be advancing fast, making solid progress with conventional designs. But somehow the little *ThrustSSC* team kept developing.

The aero-design problems could be solved with a supersonic wind tunnel but apart from the huge cost involved there was a bigger concern. To have meaningful and credible results, the supersonic tunnel would also require a supersonic moving ground under the model wheels and this was a major project on its own.

But maybe the answer to all this might just turn out to be easy. In a wind tunnel you have a static model with the supersonic air blown over it and systems to measure the pressures and forces on the model. If it's just a matter of passing the supersonic air over the model, then why not fire a supersonic model down a track and measure the pressures and forces from inside the model and transmit the data by radio?

There just happened to be such a military track in the UK known as the Long Test Track at Pendine, South Wales. Ron had a brilliant meeting with the Pendine Superintendent, who made it clear that he wanted to try something different for the track to enlarge the market for its services and that he had some 200 two-inch strafing rockets that were approaching time expiry and were no use to him. There was the possibility of developing a new supersonic aero-research capability for the track unit — so he approved.

Glynne also had a smart, low-cost solution to his rear-wheel steer. He took his brother-in-law's retired Mini and cleverly engineered a major structural extension on the back to convert it to rear-wheel steer, so that the car had the exact same wheel planform ratio as *ThrustSSC*.

We all tried the car at the MIRA test establishment and it turned out to be remarkably safe and stable to drive, even at 90mph. Glynne gave us the courage to progress with what could have been a show-stopper.

The rocket tests were a huge success. The model was accelerated by 18 rockets and reached 820mph in just 0.8 seconds. But the first run was a real lesson: the carbon-fibre model exploded into fragments as the supersonic air breached one of its construction joints. That day we had a sponsor representative with us on site and he quietly walked away convinced that the project was over.

All we had to do was to make the next rocket models in solid aluminium, but this was a warning message of what would happen to the real car if the bodywork were to be breached. Nothing could be taken for granted with extreme supersonic performance.

At the end of the rocket test programme, Ron had comparable research data from both the CFD activity at Swansea and some 13 rocket test runs. He took the data sets back to his home in south London and started work on the comparisons. He had never set out to achieve an aerodynamic solution to *ThrustSSC*: his approach had always been to review the project data and to act as an unbiased judge. We all knew something interesting was developing because he called in one of the sponsor's engineers to check his calculations. The news leaked out. Ron was faced with a straight-line correlation between the test results: both the rocket tests and the CFD had come up with identical results — one had proved the other. We had a safe car!

With such good technical results, both Ron and I knew we could do it.

But we were in for a shock. I took our proposals to a wide range of potential industry sponsors. This was the time when the UK's largest companies were promoting their courage and innovation. The results of my sales efforts were dispiriting: there was minimal interest and real concern about the risk. As so often happens, reality didn't align with their promotion. We had outstanding and credible research results and an appalling financial response. It was going to take a massive fight to get the car built.

So we now had to face the reality of challenging risk-adverse Britain. The first thing to sacrifice was my driving ambitions: we would have to find another driver so I could focus on the all-important funding. We announced this at the *ThrustSSC* press launch in London, where we showed the two huge Spey 202 engines, the rocket test model and sled, and the rear-wheel-steer Mini. After we explained that this was something of a three-way race, one of the journalists present immediately called McLaren. This brought the news that the McLaren people had terminated their *Maverick* challenger. So now it was a straight fight with Craig Breedlove.

Now we had to find our driver. The place to start was the Defence Evaluation and Research Agency (DERA) and its Centre of Human Sciences at Farnborough where flight crew are analysed and assessed. I turned up at this home of 'military shrinks' where psychologist Roger Green was nominated to take on the programme.

Green: "It's easy — we analyse you and try to find another Richard Noble."

Noble: "You'll have to do better than that!"

Roger put together a truly outstanding programme. We would announce the driver search at the press launch, review applicants' IQ and stability capabilities, stress them up in a 24-hour heated laboratory, check their driving and control skills, and then assess their teamwork skills. We had to keep the number of applicants down to sensible numbers and weed out candidates at every stage of the six-month programme. This was a self-selection programme — there was to be no presiding assessment committee.

We had announced that I wasn't driving at the press launch and the media would be encouraged to find us driver candidates. This was to work extraordinarily well.

At the time of the press launch, the PR agency were the first line of defence and all 30 applicants were directed to them. The PR team were encouraged to be strongly negative toward each individual, as an assessment of determination. This went badly wrong when one of the leading Eurofighter test pilots applied and was earnestly advised not to give up his day job! Sixteen generous candidates gave up their time to compete and gradually worked themselves through the four-stage programme.

Key to all this was the analysis of driving and controlling skills, which followed the IQ, stress and personality tests carried out in the Centre's laboratories in Farnborough. After the first session Roger Green reported that the 16 had demonstrated the highest collective IQ the Centre had ever seen. But the driving test was to be very different.

For the driving test we whittled our candidates down to five, three of whom were serving RAF pilots. To avoid the possibility of any of them carrying out their own reconnaissance of the test site, a muddy figure-of-eight rally track near Saltburn in Yorkshire, we mustered them at a hotel 100 miles away. Volkswagen were our sponsor, providing Golf rally cars and national rally champion Russell Brookes as instructor and judge.

Paul Buckett at Volkswagen had an extraordinary problem on his hands. He wanted to bring key media to Saltburn to witness the tests, but in view of our absolute security he wasn't able to tell them what it was about and where they were going — they just had to turn up at Stansted airport to join the Volkswagen plane for the flight north. The journalists in general were very trusting but one or two of the more well-known ones decided they were not joining unless they were told. Paul, being a great negotiator, somehow managed to get them aboard without revealing the plot.

The plane landed at Teesside airport and the journalists were accommodated in the airport hotel. On reaching their rooms, they each found a set of driving goggles, a white silk scarf, a stopwatch, an expanding tape measure and a small phial of an evil-smelling pale yellow liquid — which turned out to be jet fuel. By this stage the journalists were totally and absolutely confused.

We broke the news after dinner — and the party were amazed and excited by the entire plan. The atmosphere was of great humour and eager anticipation. Seeing their high levels of interest, we showed them videos and films of World Land Speed Record events and this, together with the open bar, went on until 3am. This left us just two hours' sleep before the start of the next day's activity.

The driver-evaluation programme was brilliant. Each candidate had to complete four laps of the track under supervision from Russell. That was then followed by three timed laps during which a spin meant disqualification. The candidates were not able to view each other's performance.

Although Andy Green was not the fastest, Russell was very impressed with his capability. He never missed a gear change and always kept the engine in the correct rev range; he started slowly and went faster with each lap, and had the best mechanical sympathy. The fastest driver, by contrast, was on the ragged edge of survivability and Russell was not so impressed.

The next fascinating part of this was Roger Green's teamwork decider.

Teamwork is crucial. The engineers and the logistics, communications and financial people would have to go through personal hell to get the first ever supersonic record — and the driver's role in all this would be critical. If the team were to get the message that all they were doing was to make one person a superstar with massive earning potential, then team and project might not survive the experience.

Following Saltburn, the Farnborough people invited the remaining candidates, four of them now, to review the project and evaluate its chances of success — and to design the car's cockpit. They were given contact details for all the team members and their proposal papers had to be delivered to Ron Ayers's home by midnight one cold night in January 1995.

Beautifully presented and closely argued documentation came through Ron's letterbox and we felt really bad about consigning all of it unread to the filing cabinet. Roger's plan was a smart double deception. The candidates thought they were assessing the project and the team members gave their time willingly to help them in their judgement. So on completion of the assessment tasks, the team members were surprised to get a complex questionnaire from Roger the next day asking them to assess the four final candidates. The team chose Andy Green. None of this could have been achieved without Roger's experience, innovation and enthusiasm.

Tube Investments was our first main sponsor; they

were to provide the special Reynolds 735 tube steel for the car frame and the finance to build the structure. We started build at GForce in Fontwell, Sussex and it was only then, as the huge frame came together, that we realised the sheer scale of what we were taking on. We had good research, two good engines, a great team, steel and money for the frame — what more could we want? Well, a hell of a lot as it turned out.

The immediate question was what would happen when the frame was complete and the frame sponsor's money had been spent? Would the project have to stop?

There seemed to be a ray of light. Ford were showing interest and the message coming back was that the board were enthusiastic. The Ford director driving the deal was off on an extended holiday and we would have to wait until he got back. GForce were forging ahead and we all took comfort from the fact that Ford had sponsored 'The Big Race' with us. We would all have to hang on and bite our nails.

The call came as I was driving down the M4.

"Sorry, Richard. The board has declined."

The surprising thing about rejections is that they always end with… "Is that all right?"

I pulled over to the side of the road and called John, the NatWest bank manager.

"I'm sorry, but Ford have declined. We're up against the overdraft limit. We have no more funds and I can't pay GForce. Both companies are in trouble."

Both *ThrustSSC* and GForce were NatWest customers.

I'll never, ever forget the response.

"Richard, please write the cheque. I am instructing you to write the cheque."

I called James Morton at GForce.

"Ford has declined but the bank have told me to issue the cheque. It will be with you tomorrow first thing. I suggest an immediate clearance."

The cheque was honoured by NatWest and both companies were saved.

I was having trouble with Ron. He had been 'got at' by the Department of Trade & Industry.

They had told him that they would consider a 20 per cent government grant towards building the car. After the ARV and *Atlantic Sprinter* experiences of hopeless discussions with government bodies, I had little confidence in government funding of new technology. But Ron was insistent, so we went to the DTI's Victoria Street offices in London and, sure enough, they were talking of a 20 per cent grant. Once outside in the street, I explained that I had little faith in the proposal and didn't want to spend time on it. I asked Ron if he would handle it — and he agreed.

Much later Ron told me the story. He responded to the DTI as requested. An inspector called him and put him through an extensive questionnaire before finally asking how many supersonic cars we were planning to build in the first year. Ron saw little point in further conversation and put down the phone.

As the car came together at GForce, a few glaring parts were missing — like suspension, bodywork and wheels. *Thrust2* was now on permanent exhibition in Coventry at the Museum of British Road Transport and the city was taking an interest in *ThrustSSC*. Kelsey Hanson, working for Coventry's promotions team, decided she was going to solve our problem: after all, she argued, Coventry was the birthplace of the British car-manufacturing industry. She organised the efforts of 50 Coventry companies to make parts and I was able to drive a vanload of sponsored critical components back to GForce. It was a huge gesture and cemented our long-term relations with Coventry.

The project was being progressed in direct competition with Craig Breedlove, who was getting close to completion and would clearly be running in

1996 during the summer and autumn, when Bonneville Salt Flats and Black Rock Desert would be dry. We would have to play catch-up and we needed an 'alkali playa' desert that would be dry in the period before the American deserts became usable. We found the Al-Jafr Desert in Jordan and King Hussein decided to support the programme.

Before that, we exhibited *ThrustSSC* in near-complete form at the Goodwood Festival of Speed right in front of Lord March's house. The huge car attracted incredible attention with hundreds of people walking round it each hour. I had put an RAF fin flash on the car's tail but had got the look slightly wrong and everyone wondered why the French were sponsoring the project!

We were generously given the opportunity to raise funds at the Goodwood dinner that night and I equipped the team with orange B&Q buckets. The idea was that the team would go around the dinner tables asking bidders to write their names on £20 notes and stick them in the buckets. We were one bucket short so I went around with our youngest designer to give him a hand. A serious mistake!

The designer went straight over to the McLaren table and accosted chief executive Ron Dennis with impressive familiarity.

"Come on, Ron, put some money in the bucket…"

The familiarity stumped Ron. Could this young kid be the son of someone important? But he didn't stay stumped for long. He addressed me.

"Richard, when are you going to run that car?"

"We are in competition with the Americans. We have to be in Jordan in the summer."

"OK, well I'm going to commit £1,000. But if you don't get there in the summer, you will have to pay me £2,000.'

I shook his hand.

We didn't make the Al-Jafr Desert in time and a long letter duly arrived from Ron explaining that he had checked all almanacs and references and in his view summer was officially over — so we owed him £2,000. I sent him a cheque for £2,000, which was particularly painful because it was overdraft money. Ron never cashed it and instead triumphantly displayed it in his office.

Key to everything was the engine stock. Thanks to the SALT Treaty we had been able to buy a number of Spey 202 engines paid for by my good friend Rick Jones. But we were aiming for the supersonic record and the actual power needed was unknown. Many years earlier

Donald Campbell's engineer, Leo Villa, had made me realise the important point that you need all the power you can acquire. Somehow we had also managed to obtain two very special uprated Spey engines with single-crystal turbine blades; these could run much hotter and develop more power than the 202s. Whilst we had assistance from our RAF friends familiar with the Spey 202 and the Phantom fighters, we needed further help with installation and development.

The Rolls-Royce board ban that had been imposed at the time of *Atlantic Sprinter* was still in place and with *ThrustSSC* making obvious progress the ban was extended to include our supersonic programme. The threat was made clear to the Rolls-Royce directors — anyone aiding the project would be fired. They were taking us seriously.

One person who disagreed with the board was Chris Fairhead, Director of Military Engines, who was fascinated by the *ThrustSSC* challenge and wanted to know more. He was satisfied that the programme was viable and decided to provide help with data and research. Chris had started life with Rolls-Royce as an apprentice, had worked his way up the company and was later to become Chief Executive of Eurojet, the pan-European consortium responsible for the brilliant

EJ200 Eurofighter engine. Chris argued that Rolls-Royce should take part and for six months faced an immediate termination of his entire career. Eventually Rolls-Royce backed down and Chris's support enabled us to develop and test the single-crystal Speys on the DERA Great Glen testbeds at Farnborough. So extreme were the new engine settings that the entire engine life was reduced to 60 minutes. But we had 50,000lbs of thrust available from the two engines as back-up for the 202 units.

Next up was the Farnborough Air Show of 1996. The idea was to run *ThrustSSC* on the main runway but the car was still in a million pieces. We were working in Q Shed hangar at Farnborough and since Q Shed was under the flight path the aircraft noise levels were almost unbearable. A messenger arrived from the Royal Jordanian Airlines chalet — would I come and meet King Hussein?

My wife Sally and I headed up to the chalet and waited. Eventually the King arrived, surrounded by a posse of top brass.

"*Ree-chart*, you will sit next to me," he said.

Over the next 20 minutes we built up the most extraordinary relationship. The King's magnetic personality had the effect of building instant friendship... I felt that I had known him all my life.

The military executive posse now returned and it was time for the King to visit the Farnborough indoor exhibition stands. Before he left, I pointed out our green hangar and suggested that, since he had a house nearby, perhaps he might like to visit the team sometime. Then, with a flurry of top brass, he was gone.

Back in the Farnborough hangar, the aircraft noise was incredible when whatever was flying at the time set up for landing. As the noise subsided, we heard the phone ringing at the far end of the hangar. The call was from the Air Show Director and he was fuming like nitric acid.

"I'm bloody angry. You won't hear the end of this..."

I asked what his problem was.

"It's that King — he has abandoned his exhibition visit and has hijacked a 24-car convoy and they're on their way to your hangar!"

We had literally 10 minutes to prepare. The King brought his entire entourage of senior police, air force brass, air show dignatories, and the Lord Lieutenant, leading this eminent and very surprised group into our scruffy hangar. The visit was a huge success and as King Hussein left we shook hands.

"I'll see you in Jordan, *Ree-chart*," he said.

Graham Pierce of Heavylift Cargo Airlines agreed to provide an Antonov 124 to ferry the team and 100 tons of equipment to Jordan. The King agreed to provide his desert, airbase and jet fuel.

However, the Jordan trip was not a great success. As an operational team we had yet to bond, there were multiple accidents and many of the team sported Plaster of Paris leg and arm bandages, to the huge amusement of the Jordanians.

But the first day on site was memorable. The BBC had sent a film team to follow us and somehow they had blagged their way into the secret military King Faisal airbase, where their presenter was arrested. I was planning activities with the General there when the BBC man, a prisoner now, was brought into the office flanked by two large armed guards. The General was not amused. He addressed the presenter.

"Do you realise I can have you shot for this?"

The over-confident BBC man's face fell — this was way outside his BBC terms and conditions. He was led back to the outside world a much humbler survivor.

Having totally underestimated the condition of the Al-Jafr Desert, we had to clear the section we needed of all small stones, any one of which could wreck *ThrustSSC*'s precious jet engines. Ron described track clearance as like sweeping the A303 between London and Exeter, all carried out on hands and knees. The General was mightily impressed and before long he and his top brass were clearing stones with us — this was hugely appreciated and created an amazing bond.

But early on during the Jordan trials we had an unexpected problem. The British and American politicos were competing big-time for the King's attention. A spook attached to the British Embassy made it known that he could arrange for the King to drive *ThrustSSC*. This had to be nailed before we had a huge international incident and I drove immediately to Amman to find the King inspecting a line of classic cars, surrounded by a large number of his friends. I waited at the end of the reception line.

"Ah, *Ree-chart* — what are you doing here?"

"Your Majesty, I wondered if we could have a private conversation?"

"*Ree-chart*, I know what this is about. I do not want to drive *ThrustSSC*!"

The look of relief on my face must have been very obvious because the King and all his followers burst into hilarious laughter. The crisis was averted, the friendship maintained. We all moved on.

But we only made a few *ThrustSSC* runs before the

weather broke and the Al-Jafr Desert flash-flooded. Martyn Davidson, our Operations Director, did an expert job extracting the entire desert team and equipment from what had become a very large and dangerous lake.

Back in the UK, the sponsors had written us off as a failure — there was to be no more money. Why, they said, throw good money after bad? *ThrustSSC* was a shambles…

But the *Thrust* team were made of sterner stuff — and our huge army of Mach 1 Club supporters would turn up for weekend lectures and presentations and respond by buying our merchandise in vast quantities. This was not a trickle of money: it directly enabled the team to survive.

Once again Heavylift Cargo Airlines supplied our transport back to Jordan and the King again provided our facilities there. But this time there was a new problem. *ThrustSSC* had a large VAT bill. We realised that this was our last chance and if we failed in Jordan the project was over — so the VAT payment had to await Her Majesty's pleasure. We had to have success with the second Jordan operation and also pay the VAT when we got back.

'Jordan 2' was a very different experience. The team were highly committed and the organisation was now focused and strong. There was to be no evidence of Plaster of Paris. Within two days of touchdown with the Antonov we were operational. Gradually the speeds built until on May 25th Andy hit 540mph and a major bump destroyed the rear suspension, which fortunately held together and supported the rear of the car as it slowed from that speed. Andy brought it to a halt with the rear wheels at strange angles. Had the suspension totally failed the rear of the car would have dropped, the nose would have risen upwards and Andy and the car would have flown big-time, propelled by 100,000 horsepower. The desert temperatures were also getting too hot for the on-board computers and so we made the decision to return to Farnborough and rebuild the car.

If *ThrustSSC* was tough before, there was now an even greater challenge in front of us. We had to get to Black Rock Desert in Nevada and there was to be only one more major sponsorship. This came from the BTR Group, who wanted to demonstrate to the City that their new management had new and innovative approaches to business. We rebuilt the car and did multiple crowd-pleasing 200mph afterburner runs on the Farnborough runway. We worked the Mach 1

Club hard, presenting every weekend. But no more big companies were joining. We were facing the end of the project. Britain was just not interested.

We needed £600,000 to go to the US and to make sure everyone in the team knew our position we placed the percentage of budget achieved on our Farnborough building noticeboard in large numerals. We had to be away by the end of August in order to make the six-week Black Rock Desert weather window and by the first week we were at just 16.5 per cent.

This put even more pressure on the engineers. Clearly *ThrustSSC* was in serious trouble and might never run again let alone make it to the US. The engineers realised that if they stopped work at this point the project would definitely go no further and would have to be wound up. They decided to keep going in the hope that something magical might save the programme. By mid-August funding was at 27 per cent and there it stopped.

But there was real magic in the air, not from sponsors but from within the team. Jeremy Davey had driven the website to deliver extraordinary results and, working with the Irish company Trintech, he had delivered end-to-end electronic trading on our website — the first example in the UK. The web had grown to 800 pages and a vast number of followers. Now Jeremy was in my office with a fresh idea. We needed one million litres of jet fuel for the Antonov and despite huge efforts there were no fuel sponsors. No fuel meant no travel.

"It's simple, Richard. We just invite the web followers to buy the fuel — it can be done in one hit on the web."

We took the decision immediately and launched the web offer to our followers that night. The offer was $25 for a personalised fuel certificate signed by Andy. There was no time to tell Andy — we just went for it. By 9am the next day we had funds for 150,000 litres of fuel. Our friends at Castrol were amazed at what was happening: they had always looked to Formula 1 for innovation but now *ThrustSSC* was streets ahead. Castrol joined us with more funds and we could go to America. It was a very close-run thing.

Much of the success for the 1997 supersonic record attempt must go to our American friends. My brother Andrew led the small advance party working with Jack Franck to prepare the tracks. But the word was out that *ThrustSSC* would never show because the money wasn't there. So all our hotel rooms were let to American media who had come to celebrate the next great Breedlove success. Of course, this was understandable: Breedlove already had his track prepared and had been on site for over two weeks assembling his huge hangar, impressive media assets and smartly turned-out team. Andrew and Jack quickly had the accommodation problem licked: the generous citizens of Gerlach billeted our team in their spare rooms and Dink Cryer of Dodge Carson City supplied pick-up trucks for transport. Tom Reviglio's Western Nevada Supplies provided a vast amount of support equipment and we never knew the huge scale of the bills he picked up for us. The American hospitality was to be incredibly generous.

The team decided we needed to make a *ThrustSSC* statement and within two days of arrival we were operational on our track. The hundreds of American supporters who were camped out on the desert ridge to witness an American success listened in to our radio transmissions and realised that the *ThrustSSC* team were very different — approachable and very hard-working. The American team were in bed by 8pm — the *ThrustSSC* team most definitely weren't!

The Breedlove team were having endless trouble, including a wrecked engine, and their progress plateaued. On September 25th the *ThrustSSC* team had a new world record of 714mph with a peak of 721mph. The *ThrustSSC* design was working well: there was no indication of the dreaded supersonic buffet and all appeared to be under control.

Way back in 1947, George Welch, the first American to achieve supersonic flight, calmly stated that the supersonic risks were bullshit. Was he right?

At this point the media decided to decamp. After all, they had witnessed a new world record. There was astonishment when the *ThrustSSC* team let it be known that we were staying to tackle Mach 1. Used to 'media speak' and over-hyped commercial blather, they had had difficulty in interpreting the real message. *ThrustSSC* was on site to go supersonic — the name said it all.

But there was one more serious challenge. Aware that *ThrustSSC* had nearly gone airborne in Jordan because of the collapse of the rear suspension, Andy saw this as the car's weak point. In discussions he suddenly discovered that there was a dangerous void in the all-important active-ride software. Systems designer Jerry Bliss's software controlled the car in pitch (nose up or nose down) and worked by hydraulically jacking the rear suspension down to increase downforce to oppose the natural lift as the car went faster. The hydraulic system had other jobs to perform and Andy realised the software void might result in the rear suspension retracting at speed, dropping the tail — and if that happened Andy and the car would fly.

This resulted in a team crisis. The engineering decision was to run the car with the rear suspension locked in the down position. Jerry disagreed and said he was taking no further part in the proceedings, concerned that all his work was being negated. On the following run there was a massive overload on the front suspension and the car started to become uncontrollable. Without Jerry, the team had no systems leadership and there was therefore inherent danger, such that I felt we could not continue in safety. We all had a very tough design team meeting that night and Jerry and the team shook hands and agreed to continue together.

Nick Dove, who ran the build and maintenance team, came up with the solution to the impasse. Simply by switching the different hydraulic rear suspension strut pistons, he could engineer a situation where the system could not drop the back of the car as Andy feared. The alternative was remachining the hydraulic components, which would take two weeks that we just didn't have, as daytime temperatures were getting colder and the devastating Nevada winter was on its way.

October 15th was the big day and as usual Jayne Millington, ever-professional RAF controller, was in calm control. By 9.08am *ThrustSSC* was rolling. It was an astonishing experience and the 200 media positioned in the desert pen with the best views were very quiet — real history was being made. The first run carried the loud supersonic bang, which rocked the media trucks, and the timekeepers called the speed through the mile at 759.33mph or Mach 1.015. The tension while waiting for the mandatory second run within the hour was almost unbearable. Jayne cleared *ThrustSSC* at 10.04am and the speed was 766.09mph. The new world record was 763.035mph (Mach 1.02) and the car had peaked at 771mph (Mach 1.03).

Of course, they already knew that in the small town of Gerlach, 15 miles from the midpoint of the course. The shockwaves knocked covers off the school classroom sprinklers, threw plates off dresser shelves and upset the postmistress — indeed the bangs could be heard 40 miles away. It was 100 per cent convincing and it was over.

According to Microsoft, the *ThrustSSC* website became the largest in the world for just one day and even today the YouTube videos run many millions of viewings.

Once we were back in the UK, the public were very pleased and members of the Royal Family came to our scruffy offices in Farnborough. Andy was given an immediate OBE for his courage but it was to take another 17 years before Ron Ayers was awarded an MBE for his achievement. It rather proved the saying that the Brits are never comfortable with success!

When Andy took *ThrustSSC* to his home town in Norfolk, the police had to close the roads to the airport because of the huge turn-out.

ThrustSSC was bought for the nation by the City of Coventry and we saw the huge level of public support when we attended the official handover and the entire centre of Coventry was jammed with thousands of excited fans. The police hadn't realised what was happening and at first it was a scary experience — but everyone was there to celebrate with us. *ThrustSSC* was handed over to Coventry Transport Museum, where it remains on display together with *Thrust2* and attracts huge numbers of visitors. The car is safe and the museum have the job of polishing it!

The next level of recognition came many years later in 2014 when the American Society of Mechanical Engineers awarded *ThrustSSC* with Global Engineering Landmark Status — the same honour as the Space Shuttle, the Lunar Module and the Saturn V launcher. We were all very pleased with that one!

CHAPTER 8
FARNBOROUGH AIRCRAFT

*"In my whole career in aviation I have
never come across such a compelling
opportunity — it's blooming obvious."*

John Farley, test pilot

By the year 2000, there seemed to be some sort
of pattern developing. British companies were
prepared to support our innovative projects — but
only up to a point. As with *ThrustSSC*, when it came
to actually doing the deed, support seemed to melt
away as the risk increased. It's difficult to understand
the British mentality because all of these projects were
well researched and executed by competent project and
sponsor teams. Britain is very proud of its innovation
record, but much of that was achieved many years
ago. Today our American friends describe Britain as a
country that follows.

Perhaps our projects have been too far ahead of the
times — or perhaps the risks were seen to be just too

great. The trouble is that as a pioneer you can't predict the industry response and you just have to go for it. Charles Lindbergh, first to fly the Atlantic solo, made the point: if these challenges are to be accomplished, then the country has to try, try and try again until the job is done. That is how success is achieved and new industries are established. This is real international leadership and very different from just copying what sells in other countries.

But with our next project, Farnborough Aircraft, the initiative came from NASA and it involved the huge aviation industry. We decided to make the ultimate aircraft, which would be a world leader in 'distributed' air travel.

The airline industry presently grows by a compound five per cent per annum and the numbers are huge. As I write this, Boeing is held up over the 737 Max 8 troubles but was planning to deliver its order backlog of nearly 5,000 aircraft at the rate of 60 per month. But while the industry has been a massive success, there is an opportunity for even greater growth, larger trading margins and better customer service.

There is a question as to whether the benefits of commercial passenger aviation are being used to best effect. A railway has very considerable investment in track and real estate but the trains can stop at stations along the line and thus provide more travel options for passengers. But the airline industry was designed like a 1950s shipping line with terminal-to-terminal travel — and as demand grew so the planes and the terminals at the ends of the routes became larger and larger. And as the aircraft and terminals became larger, it became too costly for these aircraft to descend from their cruising altitude, disgorge a few travellers and pick up some new ones. Of course, whilst an airline doesn't have expensive track in the sky, there is considerable route freedom.

But there is an inherent problem with all this. If a passenger's final destination isn't where the aircraft lands, say London or New York, onward travel is usually time-consuming, expensive and frustrating after the 600mph speed of the airliner.

As long as passengers were happy to travel terminal to terminal, the industry could take advantage of the square/cube law, which means that a relatively small increase in an aircraft's dimensions can result in a substantially greater payload — as with the giant Airbus A380. But in recent years the public has become more 'travel-demanding' and airlines now fly to many more destinations, bringing about a greater requirement for smaller aircraft — and the end of A380 production.

At the same time we have seen more use of business jets, beautiful aircraft that enable their fortunate passengers to avoid the time-consuming hubs, but their costs are necessarily substantial. To arrive at a total cost per mile for any aircraft, its operational flying costs have to be added to its amortised annual fixed costs, such as finance, crew, insurance, hangarage and maintenance. And if an aircraft doesn't fly very often, as can be the case with business jets, then the additional cost per mile can be very considerable. Business jets are also noisy, accelerate slowly and land at quite high speed — so they need long runways and this restricts their usefulness. Jet aircraft also have to fly high even on short routes in order to avoid the heavy fuel cost of low-level flight. It is said that the CO_2 emissions from aircraft flight above 30,000ft stay there for 100 years. The environmental price is a very high one.

Just looking at the runway lengths available, all other things considered, business jets can use only some 50 per cent of available airfields whereas propeller planes, which accelerate more quickly and land more slowly, can use about 90 per cent. Which is going to be more convenient for the short-distance traveller?

For years I used my little piston-engined aircraft like a car. I could fly fast and in a straight line point to point in most weathers and there would be minimal traffic stress. Of course, if there weren't any taxis available on arrival, precious time could be wasted, but usually someone with a car would meet you. Flying like this, you quickly realised that World War Two left England with a vast number of small airfields that have low utilisation, immediate access and can get you quite close to your eventual destination.

NASA were onto this when they realised that in the US there are 15,000 airfields, 5,000 of which have paved runways; by contrast in Europe the airfields number around 3,000. A rough calculation showed that 80 per cent of the American population live within a 20-minute drive of their local airfield. These airfields are defined as aerodromes while an airport is a larger unit defined as a destination for airline travel. Most of these aerodromes are seriously under-used and therefore NASA believed they represented an important but undeveloped infrastructural resource. The NASA programme that emerged was called SATS — Small Aircraft Transportation System. This was clever and original thinking.

There were two important technologies in this: the arrival of GPS provided safe approach and landing navigational aids with the necessary hardware in the plane and thus not funded by airfields; and Pratt & Whitney were achieving astonishing safety performance with their long-lived range of PT6 turboprop engines.

In the past a commercial light aircraft flying in cloud/instrument conditions had to have multiple engines to ensure that it could continue safely in the event of an engine failure. The new argument was that if the engine was super-safe, then there was no need for an aircraft to carry around a second engine. In the US and other countries, legal single-engine passenger-carrying operation in instrument rather than visual flying conditions was being considered and tried. In Europe there was considerable discussion and some countries were supportive, but the British Civil Aviation Authority (CAA) appeared dead against what were known as single-engine Instrument Flight Rules.

These advanced propeller aircraft would be very much quieter than jets and it was thought that this advantage might enable them to fly into the big hubs at night when the noisy jets are banned.

So the opportunity emerged to develop a new type of passenger aircraft operation and appropriate new types of aircraft. However, to demonstrate the potential and make the huge inroads into the market, these high-technology newcomers would have to be very different from existing 'taxi' aircraft.

A small aircraft like this would have to make money on a scale never previously seen. It would have to be a substantial profit centre instead of a cost centre, as with a business jet. Since it would earn money by charging by the mile flown, it would have to be very fast with high utilisation and a spectacular range. It would also have to be manufactured in a different way in order to reduce the production variations in labour costs and aircraft weight resulting from traditional hand-made aircraft manufacture.

In short, Farnborough Aircraft was planning a major revolution in civil aviation, an industry used to steady market growth with progressive innovation in small, low-risk steps. In an industry where passengers find it difficult to distinguish between an Airbus and a Boeing, there also has to be an opportunity for something different. And it would have to come from a small, gutsy company prepared to take the risk. It was to turn out to be a grim task.

The model we came up with was a 'taxi' aircraft with an Uber-type central booking and charging system to simplify operation, amass market data and ensure minimal empty journeys. It would be able to operate from the multitude of small airfields, just as NASA had planned — but there the similarity ended. The aircraft would have to be able to fly as fast as a Spitfire or P-51 Mustang and have a 1,000-mile range with 45 minutes of safe fuel reserve. The commercial model was the London 'black cab': research with cab companies showed that business customers usually travelled in groups of one, two or three people, so in view of the speed requirements the plane should be kept small. In utilisation terms it should fly around 1,000 productive hours each year and that would mean 400,000 productive paying miles per annum. Early calculations showed that the cost per mile would be similar to that of a Range Rover. Compared with flying from larger airfields by business jet, our aircraft would be only slightly slower and very much more cost-effective.

So, who would buy these magic money-making aircraft that would offer fast, bespoke point-to-point taxi travel at low operating costs?

We didn't have to look far. In trying to untangle the labyrinthine airline-operating model, a number of British Airways pilots gave us unofficial help. They had started their careers with light aircraft training and had worked their way through the system to become first officers and then captains. But all the flying hours and hard work seemed compromised when they found that new airliners were requiring fewer and fewer of their hard-won flying skills. The saying was that the airliner of the future should be captained by a human and accompanied by an unpaid dog; the dog was there to bite the captain if he touched the controls. It was said that Chinese airline pilots were to be fined if they touched the controls unnecessarily.

The idea of pilot-owned, mortgage-funded, high-performance taxi aircraft operating from small airfields with a central booking agency appeared very attractive to airline pilots and there was considerable interest. They could combine their skills with their hobby, fly to many different destinations and take time off when they wanted.

Our Farnborough Aircraft team spent learning time provided generously by Pratt & Whitney in Montréal. With the legendary reliability of their PT6A engine, Pratt & Whitney Canada had begun to realise the huge additional potential for these engines and were keen to provide help for early adopters. However, they did have a problem in that providing serious support for the new aircraft might well upset their traditional customers. Help was going to be provision of data and tech support but only as the project advanced.

The famous Dutch University of Technology,

TU Delft, was keen to help. They were innovators in the development of vacuum-infusion composites technology, which was already being used in the construction of large yachts and which could help us develop our manufacturing to a point where we could standardise production aircraft weights and labour costs. We could also pioneer new aircraft structures using the composites for best advantage, rather than replicating aluminium structures in carbon. But these innovations tend to upset the certification authorities; an early example was the Learfan, for which the Federal Aviation Administration (FAA) reputedly insisted on the carbon panels being attached with rivets instead of bonding.

As a part of all this, we learned another downside of airline travel. I had lost two good friends to airline travel when they died as a consequence of long-distance flights. Before 9/11, I used to travel extensively internationally with a set of cabin and personal condition-monitoring instruments on my lap. The cabin crew were usually fascinated by the data and the risky conditions they were experiencing on a day-by-day basis. All this could be improved dramatically with the higher cabin pressure that an all-carbon aircraft could offer. The first to demonstrate this was the Boeing 787

Dreamliner. But for our aircraft, the Farnborough F1, the secret lay with the TU Delft team, which had already proved a carbon cabin and were now looking to the process of resin vacuum infusion to make aircraft in large components. Put together, a whole new market would be available for passengers with concerns over their pulmonary functions.

Progress with the project was slow and expensive. Financial discussions with city investment people in London were not encouraging. Many of them were invested in airline businesses and saw conflict by supporting competitive, high-risk, disruptive start-ups. Meetings were interminable and the world moved on. City people wanted immediate returns and key manufacturing understandings such as the technology learning curve seemed to belong on an alien planet. What I found of particular interest was the fact that the financial people offered their opinion that the business jet was superior. It took time and persuasion to make the point that the Farnborough F1 was not necessarily for highly paid financial professionals. The real market was for directors and senior management of SMEs (small and medium-sized enterprises) — the backbone of national industry.

John Farley, a famous professional test pilot and one

of our earliest supporters, made the point.

"In my whole career in aviation I have never come across such a compelling opportunity — it's blooming obvious."

We put up the Farnborough Aircraft website and from all over the world people responded. The typical website comment was: "We knew there had to be an alternative to regional airline travel and the business jet — how do we invest?" This gave us early cashflow — but this was a time when the 'dot.com' companies were not long for this world and we were affected.

Farnborough Aircraft became a dispiriting, high-risk experience — there was minimal levity and an endless search for funds to keep the programme on the road. The first objective was to get the prototype into the air, to be followed by the thankless task of certification. But we were all up for it.

Following the success of *ThrustSSC*, we instituted a supporters' club known as the Farnborough Airforce. As with *ThrustSSC*, the idea was to share the experience and invite the many Farnborough project supporters to promote it through word of mouth. There were many memorable lectures for the club from heroes such as Eric 'Winkle' Brown and Alex Henshaw and these were a huge success and a pleasant relief from the seemingly endless financial grind.

One month we decided to take the Farnborough Airforce supporters flying on an 'at-cost' basis. My flying coach, Colin Cleaver, kindly took this in hand and on the day we had three Piper Warrior aircraft available at Blackbushe aerodrome. Each aeroplane would take three passengers and the instructor pilot, the experience consisting of a series of short flights and after each landing the passengers would shift around, allowing a fresh pair of hands on the dual controls.

All flights were memorable but one was exceptional. The young girl at the dual controls was a natural with exceptional hand/eye co-ordination and Colin, a veteran of over 20,000 hours' light aircraft time, was so impressed with her handling that he let her land the plane on her first flight while he followed through on the controls. I wrote to her parents that week explaining that their daughter had an incredible talent and co-ordination that made her a very rare natural and encouraged them to give her every support. Sadly I never got a reply, so I had to assume my letter was unwelcome.

In 2000 our critical cashflow ceased to be steady and suddenly collapsed, but a friendly investor supported the company while we searched for new funds. Despite solid interest, new investment didn't materialise and our friendly investor became keen to acquire the company, which he did after court appearances and an epic Extraordinary General Meeting in 2001. All the original backers lost their investments but were keen to see the project proceed to success under new ownership and hopefully more reliable funding.

The Farnborough F1 aircraft was renamed the Kestrel and was completed under the new ownership. It made a number of international appearances and was said to have achieved its performance numbers, which was a great achievement by the original designers. But the new company for some reason was unable to proceed further and the aircraft was sold to Alan Klapmeier's new Kestrel company in 2010.

Klapmeier was joint founder of the highly successful Cirrus company along with his brother Dale. Alan saw the opportunity to acquire Kestrel and was highly enthusiastic about the design and the prospects. But by 2018 work on the Kestrel aircraft had ceased and the project was at an end.

Perhaps Farnborough Aircraft was just too advanced for its time. Perhaps there is a good reason for the airline industry model continuing as it does. Perhaps the high-performance, point-to-point taxi aircraft will come one day.

There might just be an opportunity for an uprated Farnborough F1 capable of Mach 0.7 or more, able to operate quietly from local airfields, capable of flying 500,000 productive miles a year and landing at big airports at night when jets cannot.

CHAPTER 9
JCB DIESELMAX

"By definition, a Land Speed Record project speaks of ultimate performance and extreme capability of technology."

Dr Tim Leverton, JCB director

It was 2004 and my old friend Barrie Baxter and I had been working on a follow-on project to Farnborough Aircraft, known as ACE (Advanced Creative Engineering). I had lost most of my savings with Farnborough Aircraft, and ACE was to claim the rest. ACE was a fiendishly clever aircraft design that would take the Farnborough F1 concept to new levels of performance, reliability and safety. Barrie had a wide variety of industry contacts who might be interested in financing — but we were never able to answer a frequent question.

"Look, I am 65 years old. I have just sold my company and I have money in the bank but I may not be around all that long. Why should I invest in something that will take at least 10 years to start paying dividends and that I may never see through to fruition?"

I was sitting at my desk in Hampshire wondering what would happen next when the phone rang. It was Sir Anthony (later Lord) Bamford of JCB fame. His father, company founder Joe Bamford, had had a life-long fascination with the Land Speed Record and had even commissioned full-scale models of early racers. Sir Anthony, needing to improve the diesel engines fitted to his excavators and earth-moving vehicles, had taken the bold decision to create his own engine and produce it. Working with Ricardo Engineering, JCB had developed a bullet-proof 4-litre diesel that was to act as both powerplant and also heavy counterweight for his backhoe diggers. This was not an ideal start point for a Land Speed Record car — in fact it represented a totally fascinating challenge on its own. But Ricardo believed that the new 444 engine was capable of extraordinary development.

We had a friendly conversation and he wanted the project for 2006. Nothing more happened for a month and, as I was getting anxious about timescale, I called him and explained that if we were to run on Bonneville in 2006 we had better get on with it. This resulted in a key meeting at the company's head office in Rocester,

Staffordshire, where the directors liked the conceptual idea but didn't know what they wanted.

I explained that JCB has a worldwide reputation as a quality engineering company that delivers reliable products and results. What we should aim to do was to produce the world's fastest diesel car — an achievement they could promote for the next 10 years or more.

The board delegated the responsibility to chief engineer Dr Tim Leverton, who wasn't quite sure what was wanted. So he and I took a trip to Birmingham to see John Cobb's *Railton Mobil Special* Land Speed Record car, which was designed in the 1930s and peaked at 403mph in 1947. This four-wheel-drive machine held the world record from 1938 to 1964 and was the most famous Land Speed Record car of its time.

I explained the benefit of the four-wheel-drive concept in its simplest terms. A two-wheel-drive Bonneville car will accelerate until aerodynamic drag reaches a point where the rear wheels slip, causing the car to lose stability and yaw out of line; once out of line the high-speed airflow might then cross the body diagonally and generate huge lift — so the car flies. With four-wheel-drive, the power is distributed into each wheel and the chances of wheel slip are reduced. As designer Reid Railton also put it, a two-wheel-drive car has only half its weight available for the driving wheels to generate traction; with four-wheel-drive the entire weight of the car is available.

Railton realised that a four-wheel-drive car would be safer and might even require less power to achieve a given speed. To maximise the power-to-weight ratio, Railton used two World War One aero engines in the Cobb car, one driving the front wheels and the other the rears. Weight and complexity were reduced by not coupling the two engines. The whole car was enveloped in the most beautiful aerodynamic bodywork, known as 'The Bun', by the aerodynamicists at Brooklands. This was innovation on an enormous scale.

Tim was deeply impressed by this amazing car and our Birmingham visit set the format for *Dieselmax* — but what was possible? The fastest diesel cars could be expected to achieve around 300mph, so the target would have to be over 350mph. What could Ricardo achieve with two of the heavy JCB diesel engines, which put out only about 140bhp each?

The Ricardo programme was an eye-opener, an opportunity to use the company's superb engineering capability to transform the heavy JCB engines. Put simply, the engines had to be dry-sumped, mounted on their sides, bored out to 5-litres and turbocharged with two stage turbocharging and intercooling to 6-bar (90psi) intake pressure. The only way the engines could survive this treatment was to spray the undersides of the pistons with vast flows of cooling oil. Eventually the heavy engines were delivering 750bhp and 1,500Nm of torque — each. This works out at 150bhp/litre — about the same as a diesel-powered Le Mans racer.

Tim was the chief engineer on the project and the car was to be built by Visioneering. But first there were the aerodynamics to solve. The car needed to be long and thin to minimise cross-sectional area and associated wave drag and to give it good directional stability. There was only one person to handle the aero engineering and that was Ron Ayers. Ron set about the drag-optimisation programme working with Fluent and MIRA on the Computational Fluid Dynamics and we learned the startling differences that could be made by variation of the car's ride height. But Ron's real interest was the Bonneville spray drag.

There appear to be two elements of spray drag. The first is the enormous rooster tail of dust or salt thrown up by Land Speed Record cars. On Bonneville the salt is heavy but on Black Rock Desert the dust is light, like face powder, and on a 700mph pass *ThrustSSC* would leave a huge curtain of dust that would rise to 500ft in the air and remain there for half an hour. The power to raise these tons of dust had to come from somewhere — and that had to be from *ThrustSSC*'s engines.

The other aspect of spray drag is best described on *Dieselmax* as 'reverse momentum'. The heavy salt flies off the underside of the wheel treads turning at 300mph and flies straight into the wheel-arch bodywork, where it decelerates to an immediate stop. The weight of flying salt and its speed is very considerable and by hitting the wheel-arch bodywork it provides a reverse momentum, trying to slow the car. So Ron's solution was to direct the airflow from under the front of the car across the back of the front wheels and away out from the sides and well away from the bodywork. A result of this was the saving of a huge amount of wasted energy and releasing that energy for greater acceleration and speed.

Andy Green was to drive *Dieselmax* and he reported that once both engines were running — the rear engine often seemed temperamental — the car accelerated strongly, like a jet. Maximum speed was limited by the tyres to a safe 350mph. *Dieselmax* was a very complex vehicle with electronics operating in a highly salty environment but once sorted it performed reliably. The new record was 350.097mph.

One of the fascinating aspects of Dieselmax was

its marketing. The decision was taken to concentrate the promotion on external marketing and this was hugely successful. Included in this was a considerable range of *Dieselmax* gift merchandise that turned out to be enthusiastically bought in large quantities by JCB employees — all delighted that the risking of the brand had delivered such a highly successful achievement for the company.

Ricardo's engine development enabled JCB to revise its design programme for its next range of engines. The *Dieselmax* project raised JCB's brand values, presenting the company as a high-tech achiever, which in turn has had a substantial effect on sales and recruitment.

Tim Leverton wrote us a long letter to describe their experiences and the benefits to the company in terms of PR, brand recognition and extraordinary levels of employee motivation.

Ten years later, in 2016, they were still promoting the project!

The JCB team are keen to have another run for the 400mph record — but no one has yet beaten its 2006 record! So we have to wait. In the meantime the JCB *Dieselmax* can often be seen at the British Motor Museum, Gaydon, Warwickshire.

CHAPTER 10
BLOODHOUND

*"Do you realise, Richard, that you have
been at war for 11 continuous years?"*

Conor La Grue

The Americans were stirring and again it was very serious. Steve Fossett had decided to challenge for the supersonic Land Speed Record. Steve had been highly successful in the US futures market, had cashed in his chips and decided to concentrate on record-breaking on an industrial scale. He had more than 100 world records that included the incredible achievement of ballooning solo around the world, and then, supported by Richard Branson, flying 26,000 miles around the world non-stop. He owned every single key to unlock record-breaking success — personal motivation, finance and experience.

Now he intended to focus on the Land Speed Record and as a start he was keen to develop Craig Breedlove's 1997 car. The *ThrustSSC* supersonic record was at serious risk. How would everyone feel if we just didn't bother to challenge and took some sort of premature retirement when the greatest-ever challenge of our sport was right in front of us?

Andy Green and I met in a Whitehall pub to consider the situation. There were two questions. Do we challenge now, even if Fossett might take five years? And if we challenge now, how fast would Fossett go and how fast would we need to go? It took just a few seconds to decide to challenge and the speed had to be agreed with Ron Ayers. Ron had been doing independent work on his own ideas. Fossett, we believed, would aim for 800–850mph. We would have to go faster because Fossett would be operational first. Eventually Ron agreed to 1,000mph — which would be faster than had ever been achieved by a low-flying aircraft.

From my own point of view this was an incredible moment. We had been the first to hold the supersonic record and now, just maybe, we would get the proper resource and support to build the ultimate car — a chance to show what the country really could achieve given the tremendous breakthroughs in new technology and the special British appetite for challenge. This would be our last Land Speed Record car. Perhaps we had earned the opportunity to try and excel.

A project like this has to evolve as it progresses. Whilst there is a small team running it, the project has to take account of the many people and sponsors needed to take it through to success. In the days of record breakers like John Cobb and Sir Malcolm Campbell, their projects could be funded either personally or by a small group, which made things simpler. None of us had the funds to pay for the new programme. As before, we would have to earn and live by our deals. And we would have to take all the risk — and all the responsibility.

The only way to finance the project was again with sponsorship. The original budget was £12 million but because of delays, caused largely by the sheer difficulty in generating the finance, the eventual budget was going to head towards four times that. Ideally with a programme like this the funding should be upfront, but we would be pioneering on such an enormous scale that it was almost impossible to come up with a meaningful long-term business plan. As with *ThrustSSC*, the sponsors would be taking financial risk on two counts: would the financing stand up to enable the car to be completed and run for a record; and would the car actually achieve its objective? To counter the risks, the project must be set up to generate mind-bending volumes of publicity and public engagement as the return for sponsors.

There were two early decisions to be made that would not cost us anything.

One evening Ron and I were having dinner with Andy and his beloved girlfriend Emma. I explained that the project was such a huge challenge that we should not use our generic *Thrust* name: if we failed, it would wreck the brand for the *Thrust2* and *ThrustSSC* teams who had achieved world records and the supersonic 'first'. Ron's previous claim to fame when head of aerodynamics at the Bristol Aeroplane Company in the 1960s was the development of the huge Bloodhound Mk II surface-to-air missile, which became the mainstay of British Cold War national defence. We decided we would call the project *Bloodhound* in homage to Ron, who had enabled the team to break the Sound Barrier.

The second decision was the colour of the new challenger — so we could get that out of the way quickly. *Thrust2* had been gold, *ThrustSSC* had been black and the Campbell clan had used a particularly beautiful blue, so it had to be different. As we all left the dinner and were chatting outside, Andy commented on the special dark blue colour of my new VW Golf TSI — so we chose that.

Ron's studies showed that we would need an

unprecedented level of power to achieve the 1,000mph and that it had to be done with a jet and a rocket motor. The power requirement would be 135,000 horsepower. This was 20 per cent more than the new 65,000-tonne British aircraft carrier HMS *Queen Elizabeth* — or the same as 150 Formula 1 cars.

Aerodynamic drag rises steadily as speed increases, but as a vehicle approaches Mach 1 the airflow starts to form huge power-sapping shockwaves that require a massive increase in power to keep the vehicle accelerating. The shockwaves start over curved sections of the body where the airflow naturally speeds up and as the speeds increase the shockwaves coalesce to form two huge shocks — one pinioned on the very front of the vehicle and the other trailing at the far back. To a bystander the classic supersonic double bang is caused by the two passing shockwaves.

We needed to create the most advanced Land Speed Record car ever, using the most advanced equipment and engines. The Eurofighter Typhoon featured the most outstanding engine, the Eurojet EJ200, which was fast becoming the most reliable engine the Royal Air Force had ever had.

The first key meeting was with Lord Drayson, keen Le Mans racer and the government's Minister of

Defence Equipment and Support, the man responsible for shaking up military procurement and leading the purchase of aircraft carriers and the F-35 aircraft. Also working for the Ministry, Andy had somehow fixed a meeting with the great man.

We were ushered into the Minister's large Whitehall office and sat on his large leather sofa. As we explained the project, the Minister grew increasingly excited. We waited until the interest reached a peak and then I asked him for a supply of Eurofighter Typhoon engines. This did not go down well: it was clear we had failed and, with conversation tailing off, it was time to make our apologies and leave.

But we did not get to the office door. The Minister was on his feet...

"You can do something for us!"

"Of course, Minister. What can we do for you?"

Amazingly, at the last possible moment a trading situation was emerging. The country was having difficulty in recruiting young scientists and engineers. A combination of the rapidly growing IT industry and poorly developing national education was resulting in serious shortages. The Minister had realised that this had not been the case during the Cold War years, when Britain had led the way in high-performance aircraft development culminating in the Concorde, which had excited and inspired the whole country. The Minister wanted us to use the *BloodhoundSSC* project as a vast education programme across the country to encourage interest in the 'STEM' subjects — science, technology, engineering and mathematics. We might get our engines after all.

It was a brilliant idea — so I shook his hand.

"We'll do it!"

The Minister, used to laborious decision-making by civil servants, was clearly taken aback.

"I'm not giving you any money!"

"That's OK. We will just go and do it."

As we left the Minister's office, Andy made the classic comment.

"What the hell have you gone and done, Richard?"

This was the start of the huge *BloodhoundSSC* education programme, which by 2017 was engaging with over 120,000 youngsters a year and hopefully will have encouraged the beginnings of a very large number of science and engineering careers.

The *BloodhoundSSC* project ran through a year of analysis and research and by October 2008 was ready to launch — but there was a big problem and this time it was not just money. The *BloodhoundSSC* design team in Bristol were more aware of our difficult situation than I was. They made it clear.

"It's the environmentalists. They seem to have got the moral high ground and everyone with a 4x4 is getting public grief for emission responsibility. We're about to launch *BloodhoundSSC*, the most powerful car ever built, in the Science Museum in London, and we're going to get pole-axed. On top of that, Shell has decided to hold an environment conference at the museum at the same time as our launch — every environmentalist worth their reputation is going to be there. We're set for a very big problem — do you have a solution?"

I hadn't.

When I next made my weekly trip by car from Kingston to Bristol I still had no solution. During the journey, BBC Radio 4's weekly environmental programme *Costing the Earth* was on the radio and I was about to turn it off when I realised that this episode was different. For once the environmentalists on their moral high ground were in trouble. Under aggressive BBC questioning they were on the back foot. Amazingly they were afraid of something. This could just be our salvation.

I sat down with the design team in Bristol and the subject came up early on the agenda.

"Got any answers to the environmental challenge yet, Richard?"

"Yes, I think I have. The environmentalists don't want to talk about cows!"

My credibility hit an all-time low. The team had often wondered how long the promising and ambitious *BloodhoundSSC* project might actually last and now it seemed that the leadership had gone off the rails.

"It's easy. Cows are major polluters and we need to reference *BloodhoundSSC* jet exhaust in terms of cows. All we have to do is to research cow emissions data on the internet tonight and we'll have the way forward."

The design team found it — in Canada. The Ministry of Agriculture and Agri Food had commissioned an authoritative study on cow pollution. They had simply put a single lactating cow in a box and logged the gaseous output. The results were amazing — 6,000 litres of carbon dioxide and 640 litres of deadly methane for every day in the box.

Andy is a great mathematician — the fastest in the world! He already had the provisional run programme for the car for each year and the annual fuel burn. It didn't take him long to do the calculations.

The *BloodhoundSSC* launch at the Science Museum went ahead as planned with a very large media turnout. Lord Drayson did the memorable introduction.

"You may of course be concerned that at this time of environmental focus we are launching a programme to build the fastest and most powerful car the world has ever seen. You may be quite rightly concerned about the environmental impact of the 1,000mph *BloodhoundSSC* and I have asked the team for data.

"The environmental output of the car per annum turns out to be the same as that of 4.12 lactating cows — and if you are still worried about sustainability I will demand that the team eat beef!"

This was received with huge enjoyment and the *BloodhoundSCC* team was never troubled by environmentalists. Large numbers of visitors then attended the *BloodhoundSSC* exhibition in the Science Museum.

As we got going, a big feature of the *BloodhoundSSC* project became clear. The world went into a massive recession during 2008 and the project was going to be incredibly difficult. Breaking the Sound Barrier with *ThrustSSC* had helped the project's image and credibility, but *BloodhoundSSC* was always going to be an incredibly hard programme. To make matters worse, Steve Fossett, the highly experienced pilot, lost his life in a flying accident in the Sierra Nevada mountains and his high-profile Land Speed Record challenge died with him. *BloodhoundSSC* no longer had a traditional US competitor but our friends in Australia were pushing on hard with their 1,000mph *Aussie Invader.*

But how to do the education programme, with no relevant experience and facing an area where it seemed that everything was government-controlled? The only thing to do was to wade in and see what might develop. We started off with the Royal Academy of Engineering, which gave us a good start working with Dave Rowley. We built up a small team and the Academy got us a major grant, which was tremendous. But something was wrong: the Academy were doing great things with awards and grants but we seemed to be very far from the coal face. We were not going to make much progress by just replicating conventional work and marrying it to a most unconventional project.

A study of the US government's figures following the Apollo programme showed a massive increase in the number of PhDs in Physics, Engineering and Mathematics. The take-up dropped off alarmingly after the last Apollo flight to the Moon, because, it was thought, the inspiration was driven by television exposure and the audience was losing interest in Apollo.

At around this time we encountered PISA data.

The Programme for International Student Assessment is an innovation from the OECD (Organisation for Economic Co-operation and Development) designed to rank countries' student capability in Mathematics and English. When we started *BloodhoundSSC* education, Britain was around fifth in the world, which was very creditable, but a massive decline followed and by 2017 we had slipped into the 20s. Knowing the huge internet audience we had captured with *ThrustSSC*, we were convinced that *BloodhoundSSC* could make a serious contribution to improvement.

But first we had to get an impression of how teachers viewed all this. I called Dave Rowley.

"Dave, we need to meet science teachers, lots of them. We need to test the *BloodhoundSSC* concept. It's no good being conventional. We need to understand what teachers think of all this. What can we do quickly?"

Dave responded quickly and we obtained a corner stand at the National Exhibition Centre in Birmingham for the huge 2009 BETT show (British Educational Training and Technology). We had a beautiful model of *BloodhoundSSC* in its early form and large A3 posters to hand out. The idea was to collect a large number of science teachers and ask them what they wanted for their classes.

By 3pm we had a collection of some 20 or 30 amused teachers — and we were in for a surprise that would change an awful lot of lives.

I outlined the *BloodhoundSSC* project and asked whether they had any use for it. I explained that we would be using the most modern technology and we would be sharing as much as we could on the web via the *BloodhoundSSC* website.

I then told them that we were outside the national educational system and therefore were free to innovate and try new ideas, though always keeping in mind the curriculum. What would they like us to do?

The response from this group of teachers was at first disappointing. They gave us conventional, acceptable, boring answers — they had to do better than that.

And then one man sparked. I can still see him now, a tall guy wearing a fawn jacket and grey trousers.

"If you really want to be different and make an impact, you need to share all your car data with us live each time the car runs. This way the entire class can learn as you progress with the speeds."

The group came alive.

"Yes, that's brilliant. We could use that data and we can all learn."

They had all become eager and excited. Now we had

a massive problem: financing the build and development of the car was one thing, but to add another expensive dimension to a project that was small and already struggling was never going to be popular.

I went away from the show worried and just about to fail my first encounter with the 'Wisdom of Crowds' — this is new technology for generating crowd-based solutions. How could we make all this vast volume of data available?

It was to take me three months to realise that the teachers had just given us the golden key to the entire project and I was about to throw it away. If we provided all the data, then all over the world *BloodhoundSSC* followers would be fascinated to have and manipulate the data and would learn as the design team struggled with the technology and the final push to deliver 1,000mph. It would be one of the most powerful education programmes ever. Just imagine if, back in 1969, the Apollo 11 data had been available online.

We had to do it. The *BloodhoundSSC* team — struggling with all of the day-to-day battles and the shortage of funds — were polite and didn't dismiss it, but they weren't enthusiastic. Wasn't it just another example of wild ambition overriding availability of funds? In Formula 1 they don't seem to combine education with engineering.

All this had to go on the back burner and wouldn't be possible until we met MTN and Lambo…

Two years later we still had a big aero problem to finally nail. Our early research had shown that the desired performance should be possible and Ron was comfortable that a solution could be found — but now the time had come for the detailed proof. We were struggling: the small design team based in Bristol were coming up with the car shapes and the Computational Fluid Dynamics team at Swansea University were evaluating the aero performance. Early runs were giving us wildly varying CFD results and the project funds were running out. We needed a trend that would help with predictions — but there seemed to be no trend. Of course, an innovative project like *BloodhoundSSC* is almost always in some sort of trouble, but this time it was make or break. We thought we were out of options but then Dr Ben Evans at Swansea came up with a way forward.

"I think I can see the beginnings of a trend sequence — we may be able to control the shockwaves under the car."

This was our only way forward and it had to work

— but the work involved real aero pioneering and there was no certainty. Our friends at Intel decided to back us and made available weeks of access to three of the largest high-performance computing clusters in Europe while Rolls-Royce provided the advanced engineering analysis software. Ben and Ron were on their way with a massive programme. We could only wait and hope for a positive solution. It was binary: it would either throw up a safe result or the car would be dangerous.

The solution finally lay with Ben's and Ron's counter-intuitive decision to flatten the underside of the car. Conventional thinking had it that a flat underside gave the high-pressure shockwaves plenty of area on which to act. But the software showed that with a flat underside at Mach 1.3 there would be no shockwaves. *BloodhoundSSC* would be safe.

With that problem squared away, we needed to focus on South Africa. The original plan had been to go to Black Rock Desert in Nevada, where we had run *Thrust2* in 1983 and *ThrustSSC* in 1997.

But times had changed. Back in 1997, the Burning Man Festival had been developing in Nevada on a nearby lakebed. Owing to its enormous popularity and exponential growth, it had been relocated to Black Rock Desert and now attracted 60,000 visitors a year.

With this level of traffic, the critical desert surface was no longer safe for supersonic running and a new desert had to be found.

We had pioneered the use of high-speed, tyre-less, metal wheels for *Thrust2* and proven them with *ThrustSSC*. With these wheels, which were solid and safe, the desert surface provided the compliance, in effect doing the job of the tyre. So we needed a special desert type known as an 'alkali playa' — and, as we were to discover, there aren't many suitable candidates.

Swansea University's geography department offered to help with the desk research and some 30 alkali playas were found. Andy Green set off on his honeymoon with Emma to check the finalists and eventually the choice came down to one — Hakskeenpan in the Northern Cape province of South Africa. Positioned near the Botswana border, the pan had the right length, the right surface, the right altitude, good road access and an amazing eight-month weather window. Andy met with the Premier of the Northern Cape and it was agreed that the Northern Cape government would support the record attempt by preparing the desert and making it available.

The task at Hakskeenpan was massive. It was to involve 300 people clearing 16,000 tonnes of surface stone by hand, and also required the levelling of a transverse road and embankment. This massive undertaking was to take some seven years involving around 1,000 'man years' of work and resulted in the most perfect alkali Land Speed Record track.

With Martyn Davidson, who ran the operational side of the project, I made about 40 visits to South Africa. Martyn was doing the logistics and legals with Altus van Heerden of Bloodhound South Africa and I was failing to achieve local sponsorship funding. In general the South African public were very excited by the prospect of *BloodhoundSSC* operating in the Northern Cape but this didn't extend to financial sponsorship. We got very close to several major local deals but we kept failing.

But along the way two incredible deals were achieved. Robert Needham, our South African lawyer who was putting together the huge Northern Cape legal agreement, was very concerned about the scale of public interest in *BloodhoundSSC* and at his insistence I found myself presenting to the board of the Department of Water Affairs. They were worried that large numbers of enthusiasts would travel to South Africa to see Andy Green and *BloodhoundSSC* put in supersonic runs accompanied by the amazing sonic booms. These visitors would be unlikely to have desert experience and there was only very limited water available. There was a real risk of big trouble. The Department decided to advance an existing plan to install a 40-kilometre water pipeline, which would have a huge effect on the local desert community. For a start they could make bricks instead of importing them, and they could drink pure water instead of brackish water from boreholes.

The other huge advance came from MTN Group, the largest mobile telephone network in Africa, and one amazing, far-sighted senior executive, Lambo Kanagaratnam, MTN's Head of Science and Chief Enterprise officer. MTN had always been focused on the huge young market and the MTN Foundation puts in considerable efforts to counter the very serious education difficulties in South Africa. Lambo took to heart the very real problems of introducing high-technology products into markets where education was struggling. He took the decision for MTN to sponsor our project by bringing forward a plan to set up four enormous 70-metre communication masts and taking care of the associated logistics and support to enable some 500 channels of *BloodhoundSSC* data to be uploaded live from every car run, bounced across 250 kilometres of open Kalahari Desert and then inserted into the global internet at the local Upington portal. This had an enormous effect on the local desert population, whose mobile phones suddenly had better connectivity than those of Londoners.

When we had first visited Rietfontein, the local desert town, the school had no power connection and not one computer. Later MTN made up the deficiency and provided an entire IT lab. The local kids learned very, very quickly.

But while all these wonderful things were going on, it was also an embarrassing period. Working all hours, we just couldn't bring in the funds needed. There were long spells when we all went unpaid. Mark Chapman, our chief engineer, and the engineering team kept working, all of us collectively determined to beat the British culture, which while very positive toward the project had less enthusiasm for financial support.

Every year we would have to explain to the local South African media that we were not going to make it to the desert that year. There were always sizeable deals in development in the UK and all we could hope was that we would be ready for the first high-speed runs the following year. The South African media realised we were fighting a massive campaign back in the UK and, despite the continual failures and delays, they were incredibly supportive and maintained their encouragement and interest.

Led by Conor La Grue and Mark Chapman, the team put together a 20-company team to design, make and test the wheels. This wheel-design team was led by Lockheed Martin, which spent some two 'man years' on the programme, and the special aluminium was cast and forged in Germany. This exercise was incredibly demanding but just sometimes there would be moments of real good fortune.

In 2011 I found myself giving a presentation at a major national manufacturer awards dinner in Manchester, with the pick of the country's manufacturers and engineers at some 200 tables. As I made my way back to my table, I was grabbed by one of the directors. He wanted to introduce me to Marcus Tiefenbrun, who owned Castle Precision Engineering in Glasgow and had won the previous year's 'Manufacturer of the Year' award. Amidst all the enthusiastic hubbub, Marcus explained that his plant was a major supplier to Rolls-Royce, for whom they machined the critical jet engine rotating parts.

"Richard, we have heard about the wheels. We would like to machine them for you."

It was a highly emotional moment. Marcus had

offered an almost open-ended commitment to machine the world's fastest wheels and it was now up to us to deliver the returns big time.

Later we asked the Castle team what their major problems were.

"Apprentices — we need to expand and we train all our workforce. Unfortunately, the plant is positioned on the wrong side of Glasgow and the apprentices won't come. We can't, of course, move the plant."

The *BloodhoundSSC* team set up a major educational and promotion programme in Glasgow and 18 months later I found myself presenting at another manufacturing event. Marcus's son Yan had taken over the company's management and I asked him what effect our efforts had had on the local supply of apprentices.

"It has worked really well. We now have far too many applications and the quality is very, very good — we can't take them all!"

BloodhoundSSC was developing really well with small product-only sponsors, with some 300 participating companies providing some 3,000 products and bespoke components, all managed by Conor La Grue. This represented a truly tremendous contribution to the project and enabled the programme and build to advance as literally one by one the engineering solutions were nailed. And these deals contributed great value in the sense that this meant funds were not needed to pay for these very generous donations.

While all this was going on, our rocket-development programme was proceeding in the Mojave Desert, where we had built a test stand. We had decided on a hybrid rocket, which was the safest option because it could be safely shut down in an emergency. The oxidiser was to be nitrous oxide and the solid fuel a synthetic rubber. All this was under the management of Daniel Jubb, who was doing a great job in advancing the technology from its very basic beginnings.

Key to the development was our programme of technical lectures, the idea being to present the project to as many technical audiences as would listen to us. We were looking for response, criticism and knowledge to advance the programme. We were lucky in Stevenage, where a highly experienced engineer came forward with advice.

"Richard, do you know what you're doing with the rocket?"

"No, we're learning on the job. It's a very steep learning curve and we don't know nearly enough."

"May I suggest you study nitrous oxide — your current choice of oxidiser?"

We found out more about nitrous oxide that night. What we thought was relatively harmless 'laughing gas' was capable of causing massive explosions that could destroy entire production plants. We changed immediately to high-test peroxide as our oxidiser.

The *BloodhoundSSC* part of the rocket programme reached a peak when we ran the full-scale rocket motor as a demo at our test site at Newquay airport. About 200 of our supporters were secure in a safe, separate, military-hardened aircraft shelter following the video feed. The noise from Daniel's rocket was earth-shakingly thunderous and the supporters were very excited and all cheered, but the rocket was down on power and we were worried about its safety. We made a statement: the team had developed and run this enormous rocket in safety, but we were very far away from a safe manned rocket. It was time to find ourselves a rocket partner. Six months later we were building a mutually confident relationship with Nammo in Norway.

The first big financial sponsor was Rolex, who for *BloodhoundSSC* made a special case to move away from their traditional sponsorships of motorsport, Wimbledon tennis, golf and sailing. They took the entire project to their heart and a very close and valuable relationship developed.

After four years of continual graft we finally landed Jaguar Land Rover, a relationship that started so well, but we were unable to maintain the financial and build pace and they dropped out. Ideally, we needed to bring in these big sponsors in batches of two so that when sponsor A made a payment sponsor B would be in a position to back it up with the next payment, thus maintaining cashflow pace. However, despite working the most appalling hours and with multiple agents, we just could not achieve that Holy Grail. But we were all optimistic. Were we not generating massive media exposure and excitement in 220 countries? Were we not creating everything that a major sponsor would look for — and succeeding? We told ourselves it would just be a matter of very hard work — and time.

We were wrong.

By 2015 *BloodhoundSSC* had become a very sophisticated business, with everything focused on promotion and financial harvesting. The project's 1K Supporters' Club run by Ian Glover had over 7,000 paid-up members. Their monthly visits to the *BloodhoundSSC* plant would sell out within 24 hours. The education programme was expanding fast, with schools keen to welcome *BloodhoundSSC* and pay for the lessons and presentations. More than 37,000 people had paid to have their names on the tailfin. The online sales were growing steadily and a high percentage of the merchandise orders were coming from the US, so we were exporting in a steady way. The government's 'GREAT' British branding campaign took a huge shine to the project and *BloodhoundSSC* teams were sent to the Middle East, China, North America and South America. Castrol took care of Europe, running highly professional and successful promotions and events, complete with a full-scale show car and driver-experience simulators.

But all this depended on keeping the essential engineering core of the project funded and enabling the work of Chief Engineer Mark Chapman and the engineering team to keep up the pace. We had to show continuous and real progress, not only to the sponsors but also to the outside world — and of course to our team. The cashflow had to grow: we were going to need £15 million to get to South Africa for the first high-speed runs.

The time had come to assemble the car from the store of very expensive, specially made parts. The most expensive was the huge carbon-fibre tub built by URT to protect Andy in the event of a major accident; somehow we were able to pay the substantial bills for that one. Of the 300 companies participating, an outstanding example was haulage contractor Arthur Spriggs & Sons: Chris Spriggs provided all transportation for the education programme and for our three beautiful full-scale show cars, each of which did around 70,000 miles a year to exhibitions and schools. Often the show cars went overseas to Europe and the United States.

We were demonstrating delivery of the sponsor benefits big-time but we were still not bringing in the money fast enough. There was plenty of potential sponsor interest but no signings.

We decided to try and hit the financial nail on the head. We would put *BloodhoundSSC* on its wheels for the first time and show the car in the East Winter Garden in the centre of London's Canary Wharf financial district. It seemed sensible and attractive at the time — but it turned out to be a tactical mistake for the most unpredictable reasons.

The team came together spectacularly for the huge job of mounting the exhibition overnight and the next evening was the press launch. The Northern Cape government sent a senior delegation from their executive committee and they gave an absolutely outstanding presentation explaining why and how they, one of the poorest and least populated South African provinces, were committing to this enormous programme. The press event was a huge experience, generating media exposure valued at over £100 million in terms of the cost of the equivalent advertising space.

We had, of course, mailed a few people to invite them to the two public days and the results were astonishing — 8,000 people came to meet the team and view the car. There were so many visitors that we had to schedule batch visits and the merchandise sales totalled £60,000.

We all felt highly excited by what we had achieved, but the few new sponsor prospects turned to ashes and our list of hopefuls evaporated. So we had a huge media success, a very tired team — and we were in very big trouble.

It seemed horribly similar to our *ThrustSSC* experience. While the car was a pile of parts and a collective dream, there was no risk and funding was available. Once it was on its wheels, potential sponsors thought it represented a serious risk because the next stage was to run it.

Some months earlier the Chancellor of the Exchequer, George Osborne, had been brought to *BloodhoundSSC* by his kids to see the project. Here was a man with access to the biggest budgets in the country, so I wrote to explain what had happened and to advise that without further support the project was over. The Chancellor responded very quickly and set up a considerable government-funded programme run by the Department for Business, Innovation & Skills (BIS) to review *BloodhoundSSC* and establish its credibility and its value to the country. Timing was not great because another independent project, Kids Company, had recently gone bust, taking considerable government money with it.

Around this time, in late 2013, Li Shufu, chairman of Zhejiang Geely, China's largest independent car manufacturer, was in Coventry to meet the Prime Minister, David Cameron, and Osborne for a press event to announce Mr Shufu's new initiative — The London Electric Vehicle Company. He was to revolutionise the London taxi industry with the very clever TX hybrid taxis that would replace 21,000 old diesel London cabs. On completion of the media launch, Mr Shufu decided to visit Coventry Transport Museum and there he saw *Thrust2* and *ThrustSSC*. Wanting to generate considerable global media exposure for Geely, he saw the Land Speed Record as an opportunity. He gave the instruction — contact Noble!

A huge joint effort went into developing the relationship, including numerous visits to China. I was fortunate to meet Chairman Li and we formed a very friendly relationship. I believed *BloodhoundSSC* had met its lifetime partner and eventually the largest sponsorship we had ever negotiated was signed. *BloodhoundSSC* was back — or was it?

By June 2016 the huge BIS investigation was complete and Transport Minister Jo Johnson sent us a 'match fund' offer with, as expected, many conditions — one of which was that we had to have signed with Geely. It also had a very short timescale in which to achieve the conditions. But as soon as I read the conditions, it was clear that we could meet them all immediately. This was just amazing.

That same month the country voted to leave the EU. Without stability, many British companies decided to hold back on non-essential spending and stock up on EU imports. This was not good news for *BloodhoundSSC*.

In July we met with the BIS civil servants to hand over all the supporting documents and initiate the funding. It should have been a really exciting meeting: against all the odds the team had met the conditions and the funds would be needed in the fourth quarter of the year to follow Geely's first payment. But the meeting wasn't what we expected. It had a flavour that was difficult to define. It wasn't exciting and we all came away very confused. Something was very wrong.

Geely made its first payment and we began to ramp up *BloodhoundSSC*. It was a terrific team achievement and now, thanks to Geely and the British government, we had a real chance. One other financial sponsor was needed to make the total budget but, with the government and Geely aboard, we believed this was achievable. We would run *BloodhoundSSC* on the Hakskeenpan Desert in 2017.

Or so we thought.

As the weeks and months passed, we tried to get progress meetings with the civil service to release the funds. At the rate of spend, the first Geely payment would be used up by January 2017. The government had a lot on its plate with Brexit and, despite our frantic efforts, there were to be no further meetings and after a while it became clear to us that the government was not going to pay. Perhaps we were inexperienced in these government matters. Perhaps we were over-optimistic. But the Department for Business, Energy & Industrial Strategy (BEIS), as it was now called after a shake-up by new Prime Minister Theresa May, had all the plans and financials and were well aware of the importance of the production and payment schedules. There was much *BloodhoundSSC* criticism of the government department: if they had no intention of paying *BloodhoundSSC*, then it is fair to suggest that they should have made this clear rather than just withdraw communication.

There was one more fascinating experience in 2016. We were negotiating with the Oracle Corporation board in Redwood, California. Every year this giant technology multi-national holds its huge Oracle OpenWorld event in San Francisco, with 60,000 visitors. They seemed to be short of the keynote speaker and I was invited to deliver. This was a real honour — previous speakers have included Hillary Clinton and Arnold Schwarzenegger.

I wasn't quite clear about the implications and when the time came I was in for one hell of a shock. I turned up at the huge Moscone Center with its massive auditorium, huge stage and 150ft video screens. This was where Steve Jobs launched world-changing Apple products. I asked the lady organiser how many chairs there were.

"Oh, about 10,000 — depends on the day!"

The scale of this represented something of a major challenge — and in front of Oracle board members.

I was alone on this massive stage, there were another 4,000 following on screens outside, and God knows how many online worldwide. I needed to kick off with a good laugh.

"My name is Richard Noble, thank you for inviting me. It's good to be back in the colonies!"

This resulted in a huge roar of laughter and we were on our way...

In January 2017 Mark Chapman and I went to Hangzhou, handed over copies of the correspondence and agreements to the Geely team, and explained that without a BEIS meeting we had no idea why the government payment was not forthcoming. The Geely people were very honourable and fully understood the problem. We had a lot of discussion — but, although it was never said, the Geely team must have wondered why they should continue with finance if the British government was not going to support *BloodhoundSSC*. Later I received a personal letter from Li Shufu acknowledging that they understood that the funding failure was not our fault.

Again we had to announce that *BloodhoundSSC* would not be going to the desert in 2017 and that meant our friends at Geely had lost their big promotional opportunity.

Tony Parraman, our commercial product sponsorship executive, was fired up.

"If we're not going to South Africa in 2017, then we must at least run the car."

And so began a very long haul to get *BloodhoundSSC* ready for 200mph runs at Newquay airport in October 2017. There were only small sponsorships available: Brexit had delivered a terminal blow to the big deals, so the whole programme was on the brink of collapse for some nine months. Our only real hope for the future lay with turning the government around and getting that deal reconfirmed.

If we could do that, then it might just open up new opportunities. We put together a parliamentary team of senior ministers and went for it. There wasn't much progress with the government, but to our surprise Theresa May stood up and praised *BloodhoundSSC* at a House of Commons Prime Minister's Question Time — but still there was no discernible progress.

The Newquay operation was the culmination of the huge efforts that went into years of building public awareness and support. The plan was for three days of running: a media day, a public day and an education day, with two 200mph runs each day. It was an enormous risk to run so late in the year and there was every possibility of high winds and rain — and large-scale public disappointment. We offered the tickets on the website at £60 a head and 10,000 people came from all over the country. The outcome was to be nothing short of extraordinary: the public's enthusiasm and the team's dogged determination to deliver combined to provide an extraordinarily uplifting experience.

I arrived on site on the media day and was amazed at what Stella Diamond, Tony Parraman and the team were delivering — the place looked like a large section of the Farnborough Air Show. My first thoughts were that we had got this wrong: the show seemed far too big for our guests, who would rattle around in the over-large event and be critical of overspend and over-ambition.

Crucial to the success of the whole event was the contribution of Chris Spriggs and his huge logistics operation. Large numbers of trucks were employed to mobilise the huge educational exhibition, which seemed almost as large as an aircraft hangar and which required a massive structural base that also had to be brought in. Our friend Mark Werrell was to deliver an outstanding three-day running commentary.

On the media day the BBC put the project on national television news almost every hour and our friends at

Cisco ran a live internet feed to vast global audiences — this was clearly a foretaste of what is to come when team and car go operational on Hakskeenpan.

The public day was a real eye opener. The local roads were clogged with queues of cars and as I walked into the show I passed the merchandise pavilion, which was jammed so full it seemed like the January sales in Oxford Street. *BloodhoundSSC* was delivering big-time.

If there was poor judgement, it was mine. The team had got it exactly right and this huge number of visitors had travelled from all over the country. And, what's more, they were thrilled to be with us — this is what we had been working for all those years. Amazingly, the weather held and we had three good show days.

Among the guests were the Premier of the Northern Cape government and 20 of its senior members. They were deeply excited to be with us and to see the car run after so many years of talk and promises — and we delivered for them in spades. They now realised what they could expect when the team comes to Hakskeenpan.

So the first two show days passed and the Monday was the education day. Schools came from all over the country, including almost every school in Cornwall.

There were 3,000 kids on site and they ran around the place like an enormous playground and headed straight for the huge exhibition pavilion. The buzz was incredible. The education team had done the most wonderful job.

BloodhoundSSC stood on its fenced-off patch surrounded by its proud engineers — but they were talking amongst themselves. I think they had always been suspicious of the education work — after all, it isn't normal for a highly experienced aero or race car engineer to integrate with large numbers of schoolchildren. I reminded them that this was what we were all here for.

I came back 30 minutes later and there were peals of laughter. The engineers were interacting with the children and answering all the questions with great humour and enjoyment. Again, the buzz was incredible. This was a very, very special moment for us. The whole system had come together and was working really well.

The Newquay airport team took the 3,000 children to a special safe area alongside the runway and Andy did two shattering 200mph runs, accelerating to target speed in eight seconds and using only a few seconds of afterburner, which shakes the ground and must appear somewhere on the Richter earthquake scale.

The children were ecstatic: the noise and the excitement were incredible.

And then I realised what this was all about. The kids were the product of the screen age: they had never had a real experience like seeing a close-up *BloodhoundSSC* run. There is a suspicion that almost everything they see on their screens is over-hyped or fake. *BloodhoundSSC* brought them face to face with huge excitement and absolute reality. This is what education should be about.

Overall Newquay was a massive success. It demonstrated exactly what *BloodhoundSSC* is about and what it can deliver — and of course on a very small scale in Newquay with just 3,000 schoolchildren. Once the car starts running for real and with the live data, that experience is going to go global.

At this stage I need to mention the extraordinary achievements of the Mettle PR team. The entire project's public-relations image and branding was handled by Richard Knight and Mettle on a massive scale — including the Newquay operation. The exercise generated around £1.5 billion worth of media PR, which represented extraordinary value for the sponsors. Knowing that the project was going to take some time to deliver, the PR operation proceeded on the basis that *BloodhoundSSC* would only surface when there was news to promote, so that journalists came to respect the PR side and not waste effort on lightweight PR activity. The project always told the truth so there was no PR deception and again no wasted opportunity.

The massive website was run by Nick Chapman, the *ThrustSSC* veteran, who managed the huge scale of the online programme that was being followed in throughout the world. The size, scale and enthusiasm of the education programme attracted enormous public and schools interest and had to be of huge value to the UK — where 30 per cent of GCSE English and Mathematics candidates do not achieve exam passes.

After the Newquay 'high', the *BloodhoundSSC* team was exhausted — and dispirited. No potential sponsors came forward afterwards and our potential deals seemed frustrated and ever more distant.

The only way forward was now with the government — we had to turn them around and demonstrate the huge national potential. The political team worked hard and there were calls and proposals every day — but the wheels were spinning without traction and despite this huge, high-level effort we were getting no progress. The money was running out. The Geely deal was the last big one and without serious money in the bank we could do no engineering.

The *BloodhoundSSC* project was clearly dying and it required enormous efforts to keep up the spirit of excitement and interest and turn it around. The word got out that *BloodhoundSSC* was going nowhere and people and companies began to step away.

But there was one more incredible surprise in store for us. The parliamentary team finally delivered and we received an invitation for a meeting with Greg Clark, Secretary of State for Business, Energy and Industrial Strategy. Rick Sturge, our financial consultant, and I headed to Clark's office, up winding back stairs and into an extraordinary labyrinth of offices right at the top of the House of Commons. We both stood outside his door and I hesitated before knocking.

"Rick, what do you think is going to happen?"

Rick was his usual forthright self.

"I think we're going to be told to cease and desist. We must have caused them enormous trouble, time and cost — and it simply can't go on like this."

"I hope to God you're wrong Rick — we had better find out."

With a deep feeling of uncertainty, I knocked on the Minister's door — this was the culmination of everything we had fought so hard for over 12 years and we hadn't a clue what was about to happen.

The door was flung open by a smiling Greg Clark.

"Come in. I've been looking forward to this meeting. You call me Greg. Now, how are we going to complete this wonderful project?"

We were with Greg for 40 minutes and at the end he agreed to reinstate the match-fund grant, but there was to be no immediate money on the table.

It later transpired that we had what the ancient Greeks would have called a Pyrrhic victory. We thought we had won — but in fact we had lost. There was no further commercial appetite for providing further all-important match funding and *BloodhoundSSC* ran down to its last pounds.

We decided to go into Administration. This would ensure that the car and its supporting parts and intellectual property would stay together and not be lost in an insolvency break-up. The Bristol Administrators moved in quickly and took control and a further co-ordinated hunt went on for new funding. As a team we were hopeful that the Administrators would be able to deliver but as time went on the situation became bleak.

The crisis reached an absolute low when the Ministry of Defence requested the return of critical components already built into the car. The cheapest way to extract these parts would have been to cut up the car and destroy it — the loss of 12 years' work and the hopes of so many thousands of people.

But at the last possible minute, Andy Green and I received an email from Ian Warhurst. He had just sold his turbocharger company and, at his son's suggestion, he decided to buy *BloodhoundSSC*. The Administrators signed off the deal within a week and the car survived. Thanks to Ian, the project would live on and the team would find themselves with the financial support to complete it — an amazing situation that we had never been able to achieve in 12 very hard years.

It was the best possible outcome to a very difficult year. I gave Ian all the help he asked for but this had to be the parting of the ways. I had failed to bring *BloodhoundSSC* through to conclusion and it was now Ian's project. It needed the new money and a change of leadership and direction. Above all, I hadn't realised how tired I was after 55,000 hours of commitment.

Ian and I met for the first time and he explained that he didn't want my services in the new *BloodhoundSSC*. This was understandable: *BloodhoundSSC* was now his property and with his finance the project could continue to completion.

Car and team were now together. The product sponsors had refused to collect their parts from the Administrators because they wanted to see the project survive. The money was now available and the job could be finished. With the desert work near completion, the car built, sufficient funding and no debt, *BloodhoundSSC* was in its best-ever position in 12 years of struggle.

BloodhoundSSC had been built with the efforts of 45,000 supporters and 300 participating companies.

Conor La Grue described it rather well.

"Do you realise, Richard, that you have been at war for 11 continuous years?"

It was time to take a personal break and move on.

If you are a fatalist, then the best projects do get saved when they faced collapse. *Thrust2* was saved by Trust Securities; *ThrustSSC* was saved by crowd-funding; Farnborough Aircraft was acquired by an investor; ARV Aviation was bought out of Administration.

Perhaps if someone had stepped forward and saved the Miles 52, the British would have achieved the first-ever supersonic flight and advanced the entire aviation industry with tens of thousands of new jobs. But that would have been more difficult because it was a secret project and the extraordinary decision to terminate would remain undiscovered for many decades.

CHAPTER 11
WATER SPEED RECORD

*"I should quite like to prove to
the world that the idea was all right,
provided we had executed it a bit better."*

Reid Railton, letter to Dick Wilkins, December 14th, 1952

In September 1952, as a small boy of six, I saw John Cobb's *Crusader* Water Speed Record boat at Temple Pier on Loch Ness. This started me on a quest for the Land Speed Record. I wasn't the only one: record-breakers Art Arfons and Craig Breedlove, both my friends, had been deeply influenced by the work of Reid Railton and in particular his *Railton Mobil Special*, one of the greatest of all the Land Speed Record cars, designed for Cobb in 1937 and the first to exceed 400mph. Many years later I was privileged to take Art to meet John Cobb's widow Vicki in London.

Back in September 1952, Inverness was caught up in a huge local obsession with Cobb and his *Crusader*, a jet-powered hydroplane that would still look futuristic

60 years later, and the shops were full of models and pictures of it. When Cobb went after the record, it is said that 5,000 people made the trip to the loch to line the steep banks and witness history being made.

Cobb's *Crusader* under Railton's guidance pioneered a radical approach to hydroplane design. The weakness in many designs was the layout of two planing points at the front and one at the back. This layout effectively meant that there would have to be considerable bodywork to accommodate the structure at the front of the boat and that this bodywork could create lift capable of raising the bows to a critical angle, when the boat would fly. The simplicity of Railton's design was that he reversed the layout to that of a tricycle, having one planing point at the front and two on outrigger sponsons at the rear. This layout meant that there was minimal lift-generating bodywork at the sharp front and therefore the boat was thought to be safer.

But on September 29th, 1952, Cobb was killed when *Crusader* broke up at around 220mph. Apart from footage of the accident, nothing more was known other than that the forward planing point suffered overload damage. Aware of vulnerability in this feature, Cobb had decided to continue but not to exceed 190mph. The world Water Speed Record was then 178mph.

Cobb had no interest in personal publicity and Reid Railton, the great car designer from Brooklands days, had an almost subterranean personal profile. To learn more about him, we all had to wait until April 2018, when Karl Ludvigsen's brilliant biography, *Reid Railton: Man of Speed*, was published. It took some time to get to page 773, but there it was — reference and pictures of Railton's follow-up design, now known as *Crusader 2*.

It seems that Railton was very unhappy with the way the *Crusader* project progressed. Cobb had had two main designers on the programme: whilst Railton looked after the boat's aerodynamics, Peter Du Cane, Chief Executive of Vosper, looked after its hydrodynamics and construction at his company. It was understandable that the two designers could not agree on the hydraulic loading on *Crusader*'s planing points; the boat was totally innovative and designed for speeds that had never been achieved before. Railton, convinced of the need to toughen up the boat, had designed additional internal structure to take care of the loads, but for some reason this extra structure was not included in the build. It didn't help that Railton was working in the US and could only visit the UK occasionally and, of course, by sea.

Railton's response to the failure of the project and the loss of his friend John Cobb was to throw himself into the design of a follow-up Water Speed Record contender to prove his design. He now had all the invaluable operational experience from *Crusader* and it took him some eight months in California to design *Crusader 2*.

George Eyston, a 1930s Land Speed Record breaker who served as Cobb's operations manager at Loch Ness, supported Railton's effort. With the design reaching maturity, Railton and Eyston commissioned the making of an expensive wind-tunnel model in conditions of great secrecy at the National Physical Laboratory in Teddington, Middlesex. There was also a lightweight water tank test model.

But the story goes that money could not be found for the full-scale build of *Crusader 2*. Eyston wanted to get back to cars and the next water-speed initiative with Donald Campbell and the famous *Bluebird* K7 jet hydroplane had been given the only available funds.

No one is quite sure what happened to the models but it seems that the tank test model never left its box for some 60 years, possibly stored in Eyston's Winchester home in Sleepers Hill. It is said to have been bought by an antiques dealer and even found its way onto eBay — but there were no takers. But Land Speed Record historian Steve Holter had seen it on eBay and managed to take the photos that were printed on page 773 of the Railton book.

I saw the pictures for the first time at the book launch in April 2018. Nobody else seemed very interested but I was hooked. The whole design looked incredibly promising and was quite clearly the next stage in hydroplane design. I wanted to photograph the model — but Steve kindly arranged for me to acquire it.

Imagine driving home with the model in its original box in the back of the car. The specially made wooden box even had 'Property of Reid A. Railton August 1954' faintly pencilled on the lid. No drawings had survived but that didn't matter: all the external design work had gone into the expensive tank test model.

There was no way this Old Master should spend the rest of its days in its box or in some dusty museum. Since the original *Crusader* had been expected to reach 250mph, *Crusader 2* had to have been designed for 300mph plus — Railton always set his personal bar very high. Had this been achieved, it might still hold the Water Speed Record, some 60 years later.

Back in 2012 I attended a *Crusader* reunion on Loch Ness and met Len Newton. Len had been introduced to the *Crusader* story by his wife Julie, whose father, 'Lofty' Bennetts, had been a key member of the team in 1952. Len, like so many, had been infected with the story and had built the most beautiful *Crusader* model. Not satisfied with just building it, Len had also designed and built his own jet engine to power it.

My old friend Robin Richardson, who managed the huge Mach 1 Club, a key part of the *ThrustSSC* programme, is a keen member of the Railton Owners' Club and owns a 1936 Railton LST Special. Following the arrival of the *Crusader 2* water-tank model, it made sense for us all to meet at my Oxford home. We decided to see whether *Crusader 2* would work and Len elected to build it in his workshop in Helston, Cornwall. It was to be a 1/5th scale model, 6ft long, powered by another of Len's jet engines. *Crusader 2* would be built to exactly the design of the wind-tunnel model and there would be no alterations. We would only make changes if the original design failed to work.

In Ludvigsen's book, Railton is reported as saying that there was no need for a water tank model because he knew enough about the hydro design from his experience with *Crusader* — so we will see!

As the project advances — it is 'work in progress' at the time of writing — it now becomes possible to evaluate Railton's 1954 work in the greatest detail with the help of current technology. We have to go through the sequence of checking whether the model works (if it doesn't we have to stop the programme), then taking it forward to Computational Fluid Dynamics analysis to check aero drag and high-speed stability both in the air that flows around the model and in the water that is thrown up by the planing surfaces, and then making a smaller model to evaluate displacement drag in a specialist marine tow tank and ensure that it will climb out of the water and plane across the surface.

We are going to learn a lot about a totally fascinating subject, much of which is still a black art.

All this work will enable us to tidy up the shape and develop and predict the stability, performance and engineering loads — and once we have the loads we can progress to full-scale structural design.

Is it going to happen?

Well, it all depends on Len's model. Will it work for us? Did Reid Railton get it right?

Reid Railton's design is so advanced that nothing like this has ever been built before. Without the model runs we have absolutely no means of knowing for sure…

CHAPTER 12
WHAT HAVE
WE LEARNED?

"To understand risk, you have to live with it, encourage it and accept its consequences every day."

Richard Noble

Forty-five years spent developing projects is one hell of a long time. We have, of course, learned a lot as we struggled with impossibly limited finance that had to be earned as we advanced but with brilliant and highly motivated team members and sponsors.

To achieve world records the teams involved have to innovate on an extraordinary scale, piling innovation upon innovation and accepting very high levels of risk as a normal everyday experience. It's the ability to accept, understand and live with risk that sets these organisations apart and delivers extraordinary results. Sponsorship funding is critical because it enables a project to be its own master: sponsors pay for publicity and the project team is allowed to get on with its activities unsupervised. More conventionally financed projects often failed largely because of the inability of the sources of finance to accept what we deal with as normal levels of risk. To understand risk, you have to welcome it, live with it, encourage it and accept its consequences every day. Acceptance of risk is the big differentiator.

Failure to accept and live with daily risk leads to a very sterile climate in which innovation happens elsewhere and the economy suffers from over-staffing, delayed decisions, prolonged development and severely increased costs. And this is where leadership comes in. Leaders have to work harder and faster than anyone else in a team and have a sacred duty to ensure that decisions are made very quickly so that the organisation can move ahead smartly with implementation. But above all leaders have to delegate responsibility and authority wherever possible with the objective of getting the organisation working really fast and effectively on a wide scale.

So this book is really about the interface between risk takers and risk avoiders — and it's at this interface where small, fast-moving projects can get into difficulty.

It makes interesting reading to review the various projects for which we sought British government participation — the risk takers versus the risk avoiders. The ARV Super2 turned out to be one of the best handling of its generation of light aircraft but there was to be no government support. The word on the street was that government grants went only to the PLCs because small companies were seen as too risky and unimportant. Although the French government supported the Robin company with its competitive ATL aeroplane and over 130 were sold, many pilots thought that our Super2 was far superior.

The *Atlantic Sprinter* hull form and Ove Arup monocoque structure could have revolutionised high-speed ship development and the shape was tested in the most respected marine research unit in Europe. The government's Department of Trade & Industry (DTI), tasked with financial support for marine innovation, showed no interest. Later the managing director of Vosper admitted that his company had made a bad decision in turning us down.

The DTI even failed to understand the *ThrustSSC* project and Ron Ayers broke off discussions in exasperation.

With *BloodhoundSSC*, the UK Government did supply generous education and development grants, which had a great impact on the project's ability to build our huge STEM programme, but sadly the government's failure to advance its 2016 grant offer — when we believed the conditions had been met — lost us our main sponsor. Whilst the Secretary of State's decision to reactivate the grant 18 months later was a most welcome confirmation and correction, it was too late to save the company.

A very considerable number of *BloodhoundSSC* presentations were made to the boards of large companies and it became noticeable that many of these hierarchical organisations had little appetite for or experience of innovation. Thus we found ourselves explaining the benefits to many inexperienced listeners who were never going to take the risk. Sponsorship was often seen as merely applying the sponsor's brand to the sides of the car and benefiting from hospitality, whereas full participation could release so many more valuable benefits on a huge scale.

But there were amazing examples of how to implement sponsorships. The Initial Services and JCB deals changed the face of the companies; Castrol and Rolex showed how to promote *BloodhoundSSC*; Rolls-Royce made a huge technical contribution and gave major support to the education team; we enjoyed our short-term relationship with Jaguar Land Rover which gave us a considerable credibility boost. But the Geely contract was by far the greatest of the opportunities, involving *BloodhoundSSC* promotion right across Greater China.

As a result of Swansea University's huge input into *ThrustSSC*, they received many aero research contracts from airlines and manufacturers. Following on with *BloodhoundSSC*, they experienced large numbers of students joining for Engineering and Aerodynamics courses, many from the US and directly attributable to *BloodhoundSSC*.

But the greatest benefit is yet to come: the Northern Cape and MTN deals could turn on the whole of South Africa, where there is considerable interest along with serious educational difficulties. With luck this will still happen and repay the Northern Cape government and MTN for their enormous 1,000-man-year contribution to the development of the finest Land Speed Record course anywhere — at Hakskeenpan.

Of course, finance has always been a major problem. Like many, I am not quite sure why this should be. The UK is a wealthy economy and there is plenty of funding about — so the difficulty must be due to those who control it. One day I hope the huge benefits of these projects will be understood and subsequent ventures will be properly financed.

Facing the problems of under-financing, we evolved ways to mitigate the difficulties. Abraham Maslow came up with the solution in 1941 — simply to power up team motivation to what he called 'Self Actualisation' level. Put simply, traditional hierarchical companies find great difficulty in trusting their employees with both responsibility and authority. The responsibility is given to the employee but the authority remains further up the pyramid, so that the employee is always reporting to someone. Maslow understood that if you delegate both responsibility and appropriate authority, the recipients find themselves in situations where they can really stretch their capabilities and reach Maslow's Self Actualisation level — a level of personal status where achievers can find out who they are and demonstrate what they really can achieve. Personal motivation reaches sky-high levels and teams can achieve extraordinary deliveries of rapid innovation and achievement. During the *ThrustSSC* project we had to stop people working on Sundays as there was a real danger of burn-out. Seeing employees or contractors change dramatically once they were in the team was one of the great pleasures of the projects.

But the biggest lesson in all this was *BloodhoundSSC* education. The British education system is tightly controlled by government with an intense public stairway of curriculums, exams and school performance charts. According to the OECD's PISA (Programme for International Student Assessment) results, however, British educational achievement is less than satisfactory and the country's ranking has plunged to lower levels. During *BloodhoundSSC* we experienced schoolchildren learning by rote in order to pass exams. A secondary impact is the dependence on video screens versus reality. Almost everything can be fixed or faked on screen — but it's much more difficult to achieve that in reality. A Land Speed Record with its life-or-death implications is as close as you can probably come to extreme reality. We saw all that demonstrated at the extraordinary education day in Newquay, where we had 3,000 schoolchildren on the airfield to experience *BloodhoundSSC* runs.

One of the most important elements of education we learned was from Albert Einstein: "The only thing that interferes with my learning is my education." With *BloodhoundSSC* we learned that the crucial need is to provide the next generation with up-to-the-minute science and technology education and not to constrain them with standardised and outdated knowledge from the past.

Teachers told us how to do it: make all the data from the car available live to schools via the internet, so that pupils can familiarise themselves with the technical challenges and then follow the design team's efforts and decisions as *BloodhoundSSC* speeds towards target.

We found that record-breaking is driven by public interest and thirst for national identity and achievement. Of course, we owe a great deal to the remarkable record-breakers who came before us — Sir Henry Segrave, Sir Malcolm Campbell, George Eyston, John Cobb, Art Arfons, Craig Breedlove, Donald Campbell, Gary Gabelich — and generated such public interest that we were able to ride on the back of their great achievements to get *Thrust2* built and run. The public knew what to expect and the anticipation was considerable.

By the time of *ThrustSSC*, many of the older generation had passed on and we were into a new era. That audience divided neatly into Old Britain and New Britain. The Old Britain people said breaking the Sound Barrier on land was impossible and was a mightily expensive way to kill the driver. The Old Britain media decided that the project could never be achieved and was doomed to failure. They sincerely believed that most people would find *ThrustSSC*'s technology beyond their intellects.

Of course, we proved them wrong, big-time, and did our best to meet demand from our audience for yet more and more data and engineering knowledge. As I remember, we gave them some 800 web pages of *ThrustSSC* technology and our website was for one day the largest in the world. We were also the first in the world to implement a global crowd-funding operation, which saved the project and provided the aircraft fuel budget.

The Americans recognised the achievement with the award of Global Engineering Landmark Status by the American Society of Mechanical Engineers.

But, as usual, Britain was to disappoint. The authorities made no use of the achievement and it took a further 17 years before they finally recognised the contribution of Ron Ayers. Of course, this rather grudging approach must hide some very odd national cultural or personality traits.

If that's the case, this approach doesn't represent the people any more: many of Coventry Transport Museum's 400,000 visitors a year come to see *ThrustSSC* and 37,000 people put their names on the tail of *BloodhoundSSC*. There must be some considerable voting power there.

If you ask any of the *ThrustSSC* team why they

put so much personal effort into breaking the Sound Barrier, they will tell you: "Because we wanted to show the world what Britain can do when it sets its mind on high achievement and this was our contribution with our personal skills."

Of course, these projects are all about outstanding teamwork and, as a homage to the *ThrustSSC* team, we prefaced the website with the memorable words of Theodore Roosevelt, who really understood what all this is about:

It is not the critic who counts; not the man who points out where the strong man stumbled or where the doer of deeds could have done them better. The credit belongs to the man who is actually in the arena, whose face is marred with dust and sweat and blood. At best, he knows the triumph of high achievement; if he fails, at least he fails while daring greatly, so that his place shall never be with those cold and timid souls who knew neither victory nor defeat.

Theodore Roosevelt, Citizenship in a Republic
Paris, April 23rd, 1910

INDEX

INDEX